PRAISE FOR *BLOGGING FOR BUSINESS*

"If you've ever wondered what's the buzz about blogs, look no further than the book at hand. Blogging for Business is a textbook on the who, what, how, and why of blogs. Read it now."

MARK HUGHES, CEO AND AUTHOR OF BUZZMARKETING: GET PEOPLE TO TALK ABOUT YOUR STUFF

*"*Blogging for Business *will do for blogging what Peter Drucker's* Effective Executive *did for managerial culture. All marketing personnel, CEOs, and aspiring CEOs will rely on this book for generations to come."*

GENE J. KOPROWSKI, COLUMNIST, UNITED PRESS INTERNATIONAL

*"*Blogging for Business *is a must-read for any 21st century communicator. Holtz and Demopoulos take a big-picture strategic approach and talk about how blogging can impact your business. Best of all is the detailed section on how to measure that impact and make better decisions going forward on how to improve the effectiveness of your blogging efforts."*

KATIE DELAHAYE PAINE, PUBLISHER, THE MEASUREMENT STANDARD

"Many business owners haven't realized blogs put a human face on a faceless company. Blogs are a serious business tool with customer relations and marketing functions, traffic considerations, and direct revenue streams. Shel Holtz and Ted Demopoulos provide clearly written and practical advice, hands-on strategies, and numerous resources to make your blog one of the success stories."

SHEL HOROWITZ, BLOGGER AND AUTHOR OF
PRINCIPLED PROFIT: MARKETING THAT PUTS PEOPLE FIRST

*"*Blogging for Business *is a no-nonsense book that breaks through the hype and hyperbole of blogging to share best practices and expert insights on what it really takes for businesses to effectively use this new medium and successfully participate online."*

MIKE MANUEL, ONLINE STRATEGIST, VOCE

"Holtz and Demopoulos have a winner! Blogging for Business *shows—in easy-to-read, non-technical terms—how businesses can harness the power of Web-based publishing tools to get their message out. For business owners and managers who want to know how to make the most of this new medium,* Blogging for Business *highlights the tools and skills essential for rising to the top."*

JEFFREY M. STANTON, PHD, SCHOOL OF INFORMATION STUDIES, SYRACUSE UNIVERSITY

Contents

After 25 years in the high-tech industry, I've seen dozens of fads come and go. So when blogs became a new term on the radar, people asked me if blogs were real and if blogs were here to stay. Let's ask some important questions.

Are blogs good tools for branding, marketing, and sales?

Yes! Blogs give you a chance to reinforce your message in a positive way that is welcomed by your readers.

Are blogs good tools for customer service?

Yes! Blogs help you define and shape the customer experience with information and feedback, which form the beginning of a true discussion with your customers.

Are blogs good tools for employee communications and stakeholder services?

Yes! Blogs (especially those protected behind firewalls) can provide employees and your stakeholders with information that you can share freely in protected areas.

Are blogs easy to use?

Yes! If you can send an e-mail message, you can put posts on blogs.

Can blogs increase traffic to Web sites?

Yes! Search engines love blogs and list their latest posts in top positions, ahead of company Web sites.

Can blogs skirt around the issues of spam filters that trash legitimate e-zines?

Yes! Spam filters don't intercept or defeat blogs.

Now, add the opportunity to make money by posting ads on the blog and you have a first rate tool for customer service–centered marketing that can make money and build your brand.

In my blog, I am able to use my personal writing voice to create a tone that resounds with my clients and prospects. If they like what they read, new bonds are formed with prospects and stronger bonds are forged with existing clients. They know what they are getting—and that's good for business.

If this isn't a marketer's view of heaven, then what is?

In this fascinating book, Shel Holtz and Ted Demopoulos have described in detail how the best and brightest have used blogs to their benefit—and how you can, too.

Having the perspective of a quarter of a century in the online services world, I can safely say that if you're not blogging, you're missing an important piece of the action.

Dan Janal
PR LEADS
http://www.prleads.com
Shorewood, Minnesota

May 2, 2005, will be remembered as a landmark date in the history of business blogging. Before May 2, a few businesses were blogging, a few were considering it, and a few were aware of it. Many executives had a vague idea what blogging was but dismissed it as a fad or something irrelevant that younger people used to write about their cats. After May 2, there were few businesses that didn't understand that blogs were at least something to pay attention to and potentially a vital element of their communication efforts.

May 2 is the date that *Business Week* published its cover story, "Blogs Will Change Your Business." Written by staffers Stephen Baker and Heather Green—who would launch their own blog, "Blogspotting," on the *BW* Web site—the article exhorted business leaders to "Look past the yakkers, hobbyists, and political mobs. Your customers and rivals are figuring blogs out. Our advice: Catch up . . . or catch you later."

This piece was the first serious article in a serious business publication to explore the business consequences and opportunities associated with blogs. To be sure, blogs were getting plenty of press before May 2, 2005, but mostly in publications gearheads and techies would read. The focus on blogs' importance as a business tool by a mainstream business publication raised eyebrows and generated a flurry of activity. Both of the authors of this book saw a significant uptick in the number of queries from organizations asking, "Can you help us figure out this blog thing?"

Yes. We can.

FAD OR PERMANENT FIXTURE?

Blogs are not a fad. Consider the statistics. As of late October 2005, blog search engine Technorati was tracking over 20 million blogs. In his quarterly "state of the blogosphere" post, Technorati founder and CEO Dave Sifry noted that 70,000 blogs were created every day, the equivalent of one per second. The blogosphere (the informal network of blogs) has doubled every five months over the last several years; Sifry sees no slowing of the trend. That means that by the time this book hits store shelves, Technorati should be tracking 40 million blogs. Further, bloggers are posting somewhere between 700,000 and 1.2 million items every day, or about nine every second.

The numbers, though, tell only part of the story. The conversation taking place in the blogosphere tells the rest.

Ultimately, blogs are all about conversation. The original promise of the Internet was the democratization of communication. The cost of publishing content to a broad audience evaporated online, turning everybody into a potential publisher. Still, the technological barrier to entry was too daunting for most people, but enough hearty, intrepid individuals overcame the barriers to entry to lead the authors of *The Cluetrain Manifesto* to proclaim "markets are conversations."

Those who were enthusiastic enough to learn the ins and outs of producing online content tended to be more technologically oriented than the average Web user. Organizations responded by establishing policies forbidding engagement with the geeks and nerds companies perceived to be cyberspace's inhabitants.

Blogs represent the next significant evolution of consumer-generated content. Using easy-to-use content management software, blogs enable absolutely anybody to become a publisher, including the least technologically sophisticated among us. Thus, people who have wanted to put their thoughts and opinions out there for years—those who were always envious of their more geeky friends with their personal Web sites—suddenly could publish their content with ease.

But blogs are more than just newfangled personal Web sites. Based on a variety of means of linking back and forth, blogs are part of a global network—the previously mentioned blogosphere—where a lone voice with negligible readership can have a tremendous impact. It's not just about the one voice; it's about the people who read and respond to that voice, and the people who read and respond to the responses, producing a conversation that spreads—often with unprecedented speed—and that can be tracked.

Blogs are part of a notion called "the long tail."

BLOGS AND THE LONG TAIL

The long tail is a notion introduced originally by Chris Anderson in *Wired* magazine. (Anderson continues to write about the concept on his own blog at http://www.thelongtail.com.) The article was about digital music, but the concept applies to innumerable aspects of the digital world, blogs among them. Here's the idea.

A traditional music retailer—Tower Records or the Virgin Megastore, for example—has limited physical space in which to stock CDs. As a result, it stocks only the blockbuster hits that are most likely to move. Why stock a CD that one person might buy every five years when it can stock the latest J-Lo or Britney Spears CD that will fly off the shelves? If you picture a chart with x and y axes, these blockbuster hits soar up the left-hand side of the chart.

Digital music stores like Apple's iTunes, Rhapsody, or Napster, on the other hand, have no such shelf-space restrictions. They can maintain the entire music catalog, including songs that haven't seen radio airplay in 30 years. Looking at the same chart we suggested above for blockbusters, these items that don't sell very many copies represent the long tail, a narrow line that trails off to the right.

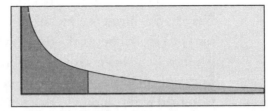

Anderson found that the digital music stores were selling as much music from the long tail as they were from the list of block-busters. While they may sell hundreds of Eminem CDs, they were also selling a few copies of old songs that, for example, somebody heard playing in an elevator, triggering an interest and prompting the purchase. In fact, consumers bought an unbelievably large percentage of the back catalog every month.

The long tail's significance, then, is that in the digital world, you don't need big numbers to have an impact.

And so it is in the blogosphere. Several pundits who haven't yet figured this out dismiss all but a hundred or so blogs, the ones with large readerships. But you only need *one* reader to link to a post on your blog to elevate that post's visibility in search engines. And if you get that one link, somebody else is likely to find your blog. Even if they don't seek out your blog, but read only the post that referenced your original item, your influence is spreading.

In addition to links, most blogs invite readers to comment. Between links and comments, blogs can, indeed, be characterized as a conversation network. The "buzz" in the blogosphere ebbs and flows. Conversations that are hot spread fast and wield tremendous influence born of the conversation. People like getting opinions and advice from one another. Think about the movies you see. Are you more influenced by the review published in your local newspaper or what your friends at work thought of it?

That's the power of blogging: people talking to one another about things they care about. If you think the ability to engage real people in real, authentic conversations is a fad, guess again. Now that it has the power to communicate, the audience will never relinquish it. The growth rate may peak, halfhearted bloggers may abandon their blogs after the novelty fades, but blogs are here to stay, at least as long as there are individuals who think they have something to say.

THE BUSINESS IMPLICATIONS

Thus, there are two implications for business:

1. *Awareness.* If there is a conversation taking place among 20 million bloggers—not to mention their readers—you can be assured that this conversation includes discussions about your business, your products or services, the issues that are important to your organization, your competitors, and maybe even you personally. Your customers are talking among themselves. You need to know what they're saying.

2. *Participation.* This conversation among your customers (and other constituents) is where messages are controlled. If you think your advertising, marketing, or public relations efforts are producing a fixed message that audiences will simply embrace, you're living in the pre–May 2, 2005, world. Your audience controls your message. The only hope you have of influencing opinions about your organization and its brands/products/services/issues is to engage in the conversation.

Luckily for you, that's what this book is all about. In *Blogging for Business,* we offer both the analysis of the blogging phenomenon and instructions on how to tap into the power of blogging.

Whether you will be responsible for your company's blogging strategy, want to start a business blog, or need to understand the impact of blogs on your organization, you'll get a lot out of this book.

Chapter 1 defines terms. Blogs, comments, permalinks, trackbacks, posts, RSS, OPML, and a variety of other jargon associated with blogging will become crystal clear by the time you've finished reading.

Chapter 2 looks at the business uses of blogs. We dig deeper into the notion of the engaged customer and his expectations, then review in more detail the implications of blogs on businesses that we've introduced here. Finally, we lay out the categories of business blogs that currently populate the Net.

Chapter 3 looks at the benefits of establishing blogs behind the firewall on your company intranet.

Chapter 4 examines the various ways you can monitor the blogosphere to find out what people are saying about you and things that are important to you.

Chapter 5 offers advice and approaches for tapping into the blogosphere. The easiest first steps involve taking advantage of the blogs that already exist. You'll learn how to appeal to bloggers so they will write favorably about your company, how to create pay-for-placement strategies (be careful of these), and how to advertise on blogs. We also cover approaches for addressing attacks and inaccuracies that appear on the blogosphere.

Chapter 6 should appeal to a lot of businesspeople. Here, we offer some thoughts on how you can make money with your blogs. Monetizing blogs is a popular discussion theme online, but don't get too hung up on it. The real power of blogs comes from engaging with your customers. Still, under the right circumstances, there's nothing wrong with raking in a buck or two.

Chapter 7 helps you dip your toe into the blogosphere by reviewing the steps you should follow when planning a business blog.

Chapter 8 provides tactical, step-by-step instructions on how to create your own business blog.

Chapter 9 will help you make sure your blog is discovered, covering the various means of promoting your blog to your audience and throughout the blogosphere. After all, if you build it, they still won't come if they don't know it's there!

Chapter 10 continues the discussion of promoting your blog, focusing specifically on the use of search engines and search engine optimization (SEO) to ensure your blogs are found when your audience searches for information it needs.

Chapter 11 explains various means for measuring the effectiveness of your blogging effort.

Chapter 12 is an overview of legal issues associated with blogs. Here, we'll cover everything from copyright and trademark to employee blogging policies.

Chapter 13, our final chapter, is our opportunity to speculate about where blogs are going from here.

Of course, what would a blogging book be without an associated blog? We'll continue the discussion about blogging for business on our blog at http://www.bloggingforbusinessbook.com, where we hope you'll join in the conversation.

Note: All Web sites shown are subject to change.

1

WHAT IS A BLOG?

So, what is a blog? The answer often given is that it's a content management system (CMS), but that description is generally not very useful. A better answer may be that a blog is a very simple Web site that has some features "traditional" Web sites will have once they mature; the mere concept of "Web site" is still extremely new. Blogs organize their content into short "posts" or articles, which are displayed in a reverse chronological order and tend to contain personal opinions as well as facts. Blogs are frequently updated and many have new posts added by their authors daily or even more often. Adding a post to a blog is simple—as easy as sending an e-mail.

HOW DOES A BLOG DIFFER FROM AN E-ZINE OR NEWSLETTER?

An e-zine, sometimes called an e-newsletter, is a document periodically e-mailed to its subscribers. An electronic analogue to a paper magazine or newsletter, it tends to be focused and periodically produced, often once every month or two.

In contrast, blogs furnish new content more often, are less formal, and often less tightly focused. Readers of a blog "pull" the content when they wish to read it; they actively visit the blog or perhaps use a feedreader. Readers of an e-zine subscribe once and have the content pushed to them via e-mail whenever new content (a new e-zine) is available.

E-zines and blogs are complementary. Both have presumably valuable content for their readers. Many organizations have one or more blogs and one or more e-zines and often find that their readerships are very different. For example, Ted both blogs at TheTedRap.com and publishes an e-zine called *securITy*. Although their focus is somewhat different, most of the content in his e-zine is also published in his blog. Some people prefer to read his blog, while others prefer to have *securITy* e-mailed to them periodically. By giving readers, both customers and potential customers, a choice, he has been able to enlarge his reach and footprint on the Internet.

HOW DOES A BLOG DIFFER FROM A BULLETIN/ MESSAGE BOARD?

A blog has a significantly narrower locus of control than a bulletin/message board, which normally allows all its users to post new content, as well as to comment on or reply to the posts. Although there is a moderator for a board (i.e., the person in charge), that person typically exercises control only when necessary—for example, to prevent chaos. Registering to post and reply on most boards is free and quick, which can lead to an unbounded number of authors. This is in stark contrast to a blog, which has one or a small number of authors who create new posts. Others may comment, if comments are enabled.

A blog inherits its author's identity and personality. Although boards do have a "personality" of their own, they tend to evolve as the contributors or authors tend to evolve and change over time.

HOW DOES A BLOG DIFFER FROM A WIKI?

Imagine a group of people producing a document. One person could draft the document and mail it to the others. Then additional people could make their contributions and edits to the document and mail it back to the group. People would constantly be wondering if they had the latest copy. The document would be constantly e-mailed back and forth. Multiple versions would exist and the potential for confusion would be high. Quite likely you have experienced this before! If the group were working on a set of documents, the situation would be even worse.

Wiki software allows a group of people to collectively work on documents without the need to download and create multiple copies of the documents. Anyone can add as well as edit content. A document or set of documents produced by wiki software is called a wiki, although sometimes the term *wiki* is used to refer to both the software and the documents themselves. Popular wiki software includes UseMod, http://www.usemod.com; TWiki, http://twiki .org; PmWiki, http://www.pmwiki.org; and MediaWiki, http://www .mediawiki.org. Most wiki software is open source.

The world largest wiki is Wikipedia, http://www.wikipedia .org. Wikipedia is a free online encyclopedia, and anyone can add or edit content. During a typical month, over 10,000 users will make additions or edits to Wikipedia. In contrast, a blog allows one or perhaps a few authors to add content (posts), although typically anyone can leave comments about the content.

Wikis have information organized according to the needs of their users. A wiki may resemble a typical Web site, a search engine, or whatever its users desire. For example, Wikipedia resembles a search engine; users search for words and phrases in its database and it returns the results. In contrast, a blog has information primarily organized by time. A blog post is most important, and prominent, when it is first created, due to the reverse chronological view of a blog's main page. It can be accessed later by several means—categories, search, etc.—but it is most valuable when first posted and most widely viewed.

Blogs are ideal for providing a flow of time-sensitive information, such as commentary and analysis of events. Wikis are ideal for organizing information that is not time sensitive. An example of Ted's last accesses to a blog and to a wiki is helpful. Ted just posted his opinions on a recent article published in the IT press on his blog, The Ted Rap, http://TheTedRap.com. His comments will be less valuable as the article becomes older and is not current. In contrast, Ted looked up the term *podcast* on Wikipedia. Its definition of podcast is as important today as when the definition was first added to Wikipedia. Furthermore, data in wikis, in this case the term *podcast,* is typically updated as appropriate. Data, or posts, in blogs are not commonly updated. Although users, including Ted, may add comments to his post, it becomes far less likely that comments will be added as the post ages. Ted may also modify his post, for example to add information or correct facts or misspellings, but this is less likely as time goes on. Ted might correct a post from last week, but it's highly unlikely he'll modify something posted a year ago.

THE BLOGOSPHERE—THE COMMUNITY OF BLOGS

Just as the term *information superhighway* was commonly used to refer to the entire Internet, *blogosphere* is a term that collectively refers to all blogs and their interconnections. Blogs are connected to each other via comments, trackbacks, links, blogrolls, and more. You'll learn more about these features later in this chapter. Bloggers tend to read many other blogs as well, thereby influencing each other.

Some blogs have emerged as A-list blogs that are widely read and trusted. A-list blogs link to each other very often and other blogs commonly link to them as well. They may have tens of thousands of readers a day or more.

Here are a few examples of A-list blogs and their descriptions:

- Boingboing, a directory of wonderful things, http://www .boingboing.net. Boingboing is a multiauthor blog with many posts a day. Topics vary widely, and include technology, political issues, electronic games, futurism, and anything the authors find interesting or unusual.
- Engadget, http://www.engadget.com, and Gizmodo, The Gadget Blog, http://www.gizmodo.com. These two blogs cover the latest electronic gadgets such as cellphones, digital cameras, gaming devices, laptop computers, and much more.
- Daily Kos: State of the Nation, http://www.dailykos.com. This is a U.S. political blog with a decided liberal slant. Posts range from long articles to short posts with links. Most of the front page posts are by Markos Moulitsas. Daily Kos has a somewhat unique feature in that readers can create their own posts in so-called diaries. Diaries are shown on the right side of the blog, and if a diary is popular, readers can vote it to "Recommended Diary" status. Moulitsas and other front page posters can also promote any posts to the front page.

- Google Blog, http://googleblog.blogspot.com. The official Google blog, which advertises "Googler insights into product and technology news and our culture." Recent posts include information on Google as well as the bird flu and recipes. It is another multiauthor blog.
- Scobleizer, http://scobleizer.wordpress.com, by Microsoft's Robert Scoble. Here you'll find many posts a day on everything related to Microsoft and the high technology industry by prolific blogger Robert Scoble.
- Hugh Hewitt, http://www.hughhewitt.com, by author, conservative talk show host, and professor of constitutional law Hugh Hewitt. This is a conservative U.S. political blog.
- Seth's Blog, http://sethgodin.typepad.com/seths_blog, by author, speaker, and "agent of change" Seth Godin. This blog contains prolific author Godin's comments on marketing, the Internet, and more.
- Dooce, http://www.dooce.com, by Heather B. Armstrong. Dooce is a hilarious blog that describes Heather's life. In her own words, she writes a lot about "poop, boobs, my dog, and my daughter." She was fired in 2002 for some of her writings about work, and ever since, the word *dooced* has meant to lose one's job because of one's Web site.

How do we know if a blog is credible? Blogs build credibility the same as any other information source. If we see an article on the front page of the *Wall Street Journal* or *New York Times* stating that space aliens have landed in Washington, D.C., and are having a summit and enjoying Texas-style barbeque with George W. Bush, we'll believe it. We will stop and read the article because those publications have earned our trust. We may not always agree with their opinions but we trust their facts. In contrast, if a similar headline appears in certain tabloids that usually appear at the grocery store checkout line, we'll probably ignore them and certainly not take them seriously. Certain tabloids seem to make ridiculous, although very amusing, claims about space aliens and other absurd topics regularly. They have certainly not earned our trust.

Blogs need to earn trust just as any medium does. If A-list blogger Robert Scoble says Microsoft is renaming Windows to Doors, we'll believe him and so will thousands of others. If we see the same information in a blog we're not very familiar with, we won't believe it, at least not without confirmation. However, trust is not confined to A-list bloggers. Blog readers tend to trust the blogs they read, regardless of popularity. We read quite a few blogs, and trust the majority of them. Some of them may have only five or ten readers—we don't know or care—but they have earned our trust.

There are blogs that cover every conceivable topic, including marketing, bowling, knitting, politics, technology, sales, software, cooking, motorcycles—you get the idea. Some blogs are the equivalent of personal online diaries, and usually of little interest if you don't know the author. Other blogs concentrate on areas that have a far wider appeal than just the author's friends and acquaintances; for example, digital photography, specific products such as Apple computers, and jazz music. Popular search engines for finding blogs of interest include Technorati, http://www.technorati.com; Daypop, http://www.daypop.com; and Google Blog Search, http://blog.google.com. It's also possible to find blogs that interest you through a blog directory such as Eatonweb Portal, http://portal.eatonweb.com; blogarama, http://www.blogarama.com; and Globe of Blogs, http://globeofblogs.com.

HOW ARE BLOGS DIFFERENT FROM PODCASTS AND VLOGS?

Podcasts are audio posts on blogs with two key characteristics: they have a show-like structure, and users can subscribe and download new content automatically. Podcast blogs are blogs that contain podcasts and supporting material, such as text descriptions. Users can subscribe using software called a podcatcher, or iTunes version 4.9 or later. They can also access podcasts individually without subscribing. Podcasts are often downloaded to an Apple iPod or other portable MPEG player. Ted often burns podcasts onto CDs and listens to them in the car. The term *podcasting* refers to creating or listening to podcasts.

Just as there are blogs that cover every conceivable topic, there are podcasts on a myriad of topics, including technology, movies, veganism, humor, religion, public relations, music, and more.

Some of the most popular podcasts include:

- *MuggleCast,* http://www.mugglenet.com—a weekly talk show for Harry Potter fans
- *Keith and The Girl,* http://keithandthegirl.com—a comedy and talk show produced several times a week
- *The MacCast,* http://maccast.com—a show for Macintosh computer users produced several times a week

Shel's podcast is *For Immediate Release: The Hobson and Holtz Report,* http://www.forimmediaterelease.biz, a twice-weekly commentary on public relations and technology with Neville Hobson. Ted doesn't podcast, although he is helping a client produce an internal podcast for employee training purposes. His favorite podcasts include Shel's *For Immediate Release* and *Closet Deadhead,* http://slapcast.com/users/closetdeadhead, a twice-weekly music and talk show.

Podcasts are a significantly different medium than text blogging for several reasons. Blogs are easy to browse, but podcasts are not. Typically, podcasts are accompanied by text descriptions of their content, sometimes including links and time-referenced tables of contents. Podcasts can be listened to in situations where blogs cannot be read: while driving, mowing the lawn, going for a bike ride, exercising in the gym, etc. Many people also listen to podcasts while engaged in other work-related activities such as e-mail.

An interesting twist on podcasting is Talkr, http://www.talkr .com, which can convert a blog into audio. Ted uses Talkr's free partner service which allows his readers to click a button located at the top of each post to have it read to them in a pleasant female voice. Feedback from his blog's visitors has been uniformly positive so far. The more choices you give visitors to consume your content the better!

Vlogs are blogs in which the main content is video. Relatively inexpensive hardware and software puts video blogging within most people's reach today. The number of vlogs as compared to podcasts and certainly blogs is low today but increasing rapidly.

Vlogs' content includes political material, artist expressions, mundane "home movies"–type video, cooking, humor, technical, and just about anything else you can imagine. There are few if any vlogs being used for business purposes today, but the possibilities are immense. Examples include a CEO's address to stockholders and employees, how-to videos, product demonstrations, training videos, and much more.

Both podcasting and video blogging are very much in their infancy today.

THE ANATOMY OF A BLOG

As it turns out, blogs are simple Web sites, or parts of Web sites, with some defining characteristics we'll look at soon. First, let's consider a typical business Web site. Most organizations' Web sites tend to be pretty boring and static, with little significant change on a daily, weekly, or even monthly basis. Internet users typically don't have much reason to repeatedly visit a Web site unless they are looking for something specific. The same can be said about a company's internal sites. How many employees regularly visit their company's human resources Web site or pages? A typical and smart way to try to overcome this scenario is to have useful information available and update and enhance it regularly.

For an organization, this usually translates into adding "free stuff" to the Web site. *Free* is a very important concept on the Internet. In many ways, *free* is baked into the DNA of the Internet, tracing back to its roots as entirely noncommercial. No one wants to read your marketing material no matter how well done it may be, but add something free that users like and regularly update and add to it, and Internet users will begin to like your site and hopefully visit it regularly. No one wants to read HR policies, but regularly add useful information on new benefits and users may start visiting. Articles, bulletin boards, news items, and product information are good examples of free elements that might add to the value of your Web site. For example, on his Web site, http://www.demop.com, Ted has free articles and a free newsletter, and regularly adds other new free things. But these interesting free items tend to play a relatively minor role on most organizations' Web sites, which serve primarily as marketing vehicles; and intranets can be even more dull.

What if

- the new and free stuff was highlighted on the Web site?
- the Web site could somehow be less formal and dry, yet still equally professional?
- users saw the latest information by default?
- the Web site was more dynamic with frequent, new nonpromotional material added?
- users could add comments in appropriate places, making it interactive and fostering a sense of community?
- all this information was archived and somehow indexed for ease of access and to make the search engines happy?

Well, quite simply, what you would have is a blog!

A Typical Blog

When you look at a typical blog, you'll usually see the name of the blog and perhaps a description of the blog, a number of dated posts with optional comments, and a sidebar that contains additional information. There is no blog standard, but this is pretty typical.

Robert Scoble's Scobleizer, http://scobleizer.wordpress.com, is one of the most popular blogs. (See Figure 1.1.) He's a midlevel Microsoft employee who just might have more influence than Bill Gates—his blog is that popular! He blogs on Microsoft, technology, and related issues. His blog has his picture and blog name on top. A sidebar on the right about an inch wide contains some mis-

FIGURE 1.1 *Robert Scoble's Scobleizer Blog*

cellaneous material, including a map and calendar. The main section of the blog contains a number of dated posts, most recent first, which contain the actual content. Robert Scoble is a prolific blogger and has multiple posts for July 30.

Elements of a Blog

Now that we've seen a typical blog, we'll look at common blog components in more detail. Realize that there is no blog standard. Some blogs may be extremely simple and incorporate very few of these components, while other may be more complex. The key goal is to have a blog to which people return. That means an easy to use and navigate blog with strong content!

Name/title. A blog will typically have a name displayed on top, which may or may not be descriptive. Anything goes. It can be useful to compare blog names to the names of musical groups.

Classical musical groups tend to have descriptive, staid, and boring titles: The Boston Symphony, The Austin Civic Orchestra, and The Weller Quartet. They have much in common with company names such as International Business Machines, Abbott Laboratories, and Toyota Motor Corporation. They tend to be quite conservative.

Let's look at some rock and alternative band names: Gay Bikers on Acid, The Rolling Stones, The Black Eyed Peas, and The Grateful Dead. According to blog search engine Technorati, the most popular blogs are named Boing Boing, Instapundit, Daily Kos, Gizmodo, and Fark. Notice the similarities? Basically, *anything* goes.

Although anything goes, you may want to be somewhat more conservative in naming a blog if its primary purpose is business. A blog doesn't even need a formal name. Ted could have named his blog Ted Demopoulos's Blog instead of The Ted Rap. In general, we'd suggest a less-than-outlandish name for a serious blog. As blogs grow up and mature, strange and wild names may become less popular, and names may resemble those of classical music groups.

A name that has something to do with the blog's topic makes sense. For example, Ted loves the name FastLane for General Motors' blog written by Bob Lutz, GM vice chairman, and other high level GM management personnel. Naming it something irrelevant and bizarre wouldn't work as well, and probably wouldn't fit in with GM's culture and image.

Description. Blogs often include a descriptive subtitle. For example, The Ted Rap says: Ted Demopoulos's thoughts and musings on Information Technology, Security, Business and more. It gives the reader a pretty good idea of the range of topics Ted writes about, and by adding "more," it states clearly that he goes off topic occasionally, as many bloggers do.

Interestingly, very few blogs state that they are blogs. Many readers don't know or perhaps even care.

Posts. Posts—also called articles—contain the content. They are dated and displayed in reverse chronological order (i.e., most recent first). New posts are frequently added to a typical blog anywhere from several times a day to weekly. Posts are usually text but can be audio, video, or anything else. They tend to be conversational in tone and often contain opinions as well as facts, much as an editorial column in a newspaper. Many blogs have new posts daily, and some many times a day.

For a blog to be effective, the posts need to contain useful content and be primarily nonpromotional. An occasional post tooting your own horn or your organization's—for example, outlining new services or products or mentioning an award you won—is OK. But even these need to be written in a conversational and informational style, not in standard marketing or business language. Posts are not advertisements!

For example, recent posts on Ted's blog include his comments and analysis on Microsoft's decision to ban the word *democracy* and other politically sensitive words by bloggers on its new Web portal in China, a review of the book *The Likeability Factor* by Tim Sanders, and a comparison of major industry information security certifications including his opinions and advice on them.

Posts often contain links, and links are very important in the interconnected blogosphere. Most bloggers would not think of commenting on an article or another blogger's post without linking to it. Anything else that is referenced in a post, such as a company, Web site, or service, is typically linked to as well. These links add significant value to readers as they can examine anything commented on or referenced with a quick and easy mouse click.

Comments. Comments are a key distinguishing feature of blogs. Most blogs allow users to leave comments in response to individual posts. One could argue that a blog that doesn't allow comments is not a blog at all, and in fact many people do. Certainly a blog that doesn't allow comments loses a key piece of blog functionality—interactivity with readers. The ability to have a conversation is clearly diminished if one party cannot speak!

A few times Ted has found intriguing blogs to which he had something interesting to add, but found that there was no provision for comments. The value of these blogs is diminished in his mind, and in general he never returns to them. Many others report similar experiences. We not only want the ability to join the conversation, but we want to read what others may have added.

Not everyone agrees that comments are required, or even desirable, on blogs. Dave Winer, for example, widely credited with inventing blogs, thinks the nice thing about Web logs is that they are *not* discussion groups or mail lists, and he has enabled comments on very few of his posts. He believes that comments are not an intrinsic part of a Web log and have basically failed. Users who want to comment can do so on their own blogs and use trackbacks, described below, if supported.

One thing to be aware of, however, is comment spam, which refers to unwanted commercial comments that are unrelated to the original post and usually left by automatic software robots. Comment spam often contains flagrant advertisements for sexual enhancement drugs, cheap software, online poker, penis enlargement, etc. Various techniques are available for reducing comment spam, such as requiring those leaving comments to retype a special code that is displayed in a slightly distorted format, known as a *captcha*. The automated software robots can't read the captcha and reenter it (at least not yet), so they can't leave their garbage spam comments.

Some people buy products advertised in comment spam; however, more important to the spammers than these initial sales is the links they leave in their comments. Search engines, in part, determine relative page rank for search results based on the number of inbound links a Web page has. The logic is that if a lot of people link to a page, it must be good! Spam comments increase the number of links to a page, raising its importance in the eyes of the search engines, and in the end delivering more search engine–directed traffic and sales to the spammers.

One way to combat comment spam is through comment moderation, a technique whereby comments need to be approved by an authorized person, usually the blogger, before they are made visible. Comment moderation is a practical technique used to avoid inappropriate comments, such as personal attacks, profanities, social and other agendas unrelated to the post, etc. In general, comment moderation should not be used to avoid criticisms or discussion.

Comment moderation is one technique useful in fighting spam. Having a corporate blog littered with a few hundred spam comments, often literally overnight, is quite inappropriate in appearance!

Trackbacks. Comments are a great mechanism for enabling conversations, but they are not the only mechanism. Bloggers very often post to their own blogs to comment and expand on what they have read on someone else's blog. It's hard to quickly and easily know if another blogger has commented on a blog post on another blog. Trackbacks were created to solve this problem and many blogs and blogging software now implement trackbacks.

If the blogging utility you use permits trackbacks, you can assign a unique trackback URL to each of your posts. When people write posts for their own blogs, they can include your trackback URL as part of their posts.

Your blog will update the original post with a link to every blog that has tracked back, allowing you and your readers to see exactly who has commented on the post and read what they have written. Trackbacks, then, are comments that are left on another blog that is linked to yours. Not all blogging software implements trackbacks today, although there are third-party plug-ins available to enable those that don't, such as Blogger.com.

Similar to comment spam, trackback spam can be a problem. When spammers add a trackback spam, they get a link to the site they are promoting. Although there are various techniques to help combat trackback spam, many of the effective techniques used to combat comment spam, such as captchas, cannot be used due to the technical implementation of trackbacks. Ted believes the trackback specification will need to evolve to allow combating trackback spam more effectively.

Permalinks. A permalink is a permanent link or URL to a blog post. Permalinks allow bloggers and others to link to specific posts, knowing the URL will not change or become obsolete. Blog posts are initially accessed via the main blog page, but blogs typically list only the ten or so most recent posts. After a post scrolls off the main page, it is only accessible via its permalink. Each post typically has its permalink following the post, sometimes signi-fied by the word *permalink* or the character "#."

Sidebar. A typical blog will contain one or more sidebars, nar-row areas on the right and/or left side of the browser window. In Figure 1.1, you can see a sidebar on the right-hand side of the Scobleizer blog.

Sidebars can contain just about anything. Typical sidebar con-tents include a picture of the author, an "about" section with some prose about the author or blog, contact information, a list of recent posts by title, links to the main organization's Web site, blogrolls, advertisements, archives, categories, and a search fea-ture. Several of these are described below.

Blogrolls. A blogroll is simply a list of other blogs. Many bloggers list other blogs they like or regularly read, or of which they approve. The blogs are listed by name or sometimes the au-thor's name, and link to the blogs themselves. A blogroll may be named Blogroll, Blogs I Read, Blogs I Like, or something similar.

Blogrolls are important because once you find a blog that is useful or enjoyable, it is quite likely blogs in its blogroll may be similar. They can be helpful for finding additional useful blogs.

There are a number of tools that can make managing blog-rolls easier. Ted still manually edits the HTML code of his blog's template to modify his blogroll, and finds that adequate, but most people prefer not to deal with raw HTML code. For instance, Blog-Rolling, http://www.blogrolling.com, can help manage your blog-roll, with features like adding new blogs to your blogroll with one click, and an easy-to-use blogroll editing page.

A blogroll could come from a feedreader. Most allow export-ing the list of feeds subscribed to as OPML, which can then be used as the basis of your blogroll.

Archives. Most blogs list the ten or so most recent posts. Older posts are archived but are easily accessible for users who want to take a look back at some of their favorite posts, need to access them for research, or just want to learn more about a typical topic or blogger. Sidebars will typically contain a set of links to older posts, usually by month or week.

Categories. Archives are not a convenient mechanism to access older posts. They simply organize posts by date instead of by content. Categories allow organizing posts by content, and each post can belong to more than one category. A blogger can tag posts as belonging to one or more named categories, which can be any topics or issues on which they blog. The blogger chooses the categories that a blog implements. For example, the categories on Shel's blog include Instant Messaging, Blogging, Legal, Media, Podcasting, Technology, and Wikis, which are all topics on which he tends to blog. A fishing blog might have categories such as Bait, Line, Fishing Poles, Bass, Trout, and Carp.

Technorati, a popular blog search engine, by default "tags" posts by the categories to which they belong. Users can search by tag name, as we'll see later.

Search. Many blogs have search capabilities built in, often on the sidebar. Sometimes they allow searching the blog, the blogosphere, or the entire Web. Several blog software products, although not all, have search capability built in as a standard feature. In addition, there are several add-on sources for integrating a search function into blogs, including those from Technorati and Google.

Syndication. A friend recently commented that there is a lot of great information available in blogs but who has the time to read them? Syndication is designed to solve this problem: it allows us to track more information in less time. Information from a Web site can be "syndicated" into a feed—a simple file that usually contains a list of what's new on a Web site. This file is read via a feedreader, which can be a stand-alone or Web-based utility, or a plug-in to a browser or e-mail program. Each item in a feed has a title, a description, and a link to the Web site where the item appears. For a blog, the items that will be included in a syndicated feed will be the most recent posts. An item's description might be its first paragraph or even the entire post; for example, the feed for Ted's blog contains the title, the full post, and a link for each of his last ten posts.

There are two competing yet extremely similar formats for syndication, RSS and Atom. RSS stands for "rich site summary" or "really simple syndication," depending on the version. Atom is not an acronym.

A list of items representing content such as new blog posts or Web pages can be defined in RSS or Atom. This is usually done automatically, for example by the blogging software, but the owner of a Web site or blog can also do it manually. This list is typically called the "feed." An aggregator or feedreader lets a user easily and quickly check for new content of interest. For a blog reader, a feedreader allows reading more blogs in the same amount of time. It is not necessary to surf from blog to blog; the feedreader displays all the new posts from blogs in which the reader is interested, and the reader can simply click on a post to see its full content.

RSS is used not only by blogs but by traditional Web sites as well. For example, the Web sites of the *New York Times,* Reuters, Yahoo!, the *Wall Street Journal,* National Public Radio, The U.S. Department of State, and the *Washington Post* all have RSS feeds. Many sites have multiple feeds; for example, the *New York Times* site has feeds for arts, automobiles, books, business, etc., which parallel the Web site's content. Even some retailers' Web sites have RSS feeds that show what new merchandise is available.

There are many popular feedreaders, including SharpReader, FeedDemon, and Feedreader, which are stand-alone applications; Bloglines and My Yahoo!; which are Web-based applications; and Pluck and NewsGator, which are plug-ins for browsers and Microsoft Outlook, respectively. We'll see examples of feedreaders in the next chapter when we discuss monitoring blogs.

RSS and Atom feeds are sometimes confused with e-mail, but they are extremely different. E-mail is a file that is actively sent or "pushed" to the recipients. Atom and RSS feeds are not sent at all, and there is no concept of a sender or sending. They are requested or "pulled" by a user using a feedreader. Confusion exists because some users access feeds using their e-mail application with a special-purpose feed plug-in; for example, using Outlook with the Pluck plug-in.

SUMMARY

Blogs are powerful tools because they are easy to use and offer a range of features that make it easy to build community, spread ideas, engage in a conversation, solicit feedback, and be found on the Web. But how can blogs serve the interests of your business? That's the focus of Chapter 2.

2

BUSINESS USES OF BLOGS

Remember all the different kinds of customers we identified in Chapter 1? Well, effective communication with those customers begins after you've clearly established the business purpose for your communication with them. What business issue is your communication addressing? Are you trying to open a dialog with existing or prospective customers? Are you looking to increase support from your current partners or preferred vendors? Or are you communicating future plans to your investors? Once you know what your goals are, you can develop communication strategies to meet them and determine which tactics you will use to execute those strategies.

Blogs are a tactic that can help you reach your communication goals. Through blogging, your company can build goodwill, attract new business, improve customer relations, enhance your brand, recruit the best employees, weather a crisis, and build support for initiatives. Hundreds of companies are already actively participating in the blogosphere, contributing a variety of blogs to the online community. In this chapter, we'll examine the broad range of blogs your company can implement.

The best business blogs were implemented in support of some business goal. Determining the kind of blogs you might consider begins with a review of your goals and issues in order to identify where your opportunities may lie. One kind of blog you should *never* launch is the "let's launch a blog" blog. Any company blog should be viewed as a part of the company's communication strategy. Regardless of their importance and the potential value they can accrue for your company, blogs are still just one tool in your bag and may not be right for every occasion. Selecting the proper outlet for your strategic communication is the last step in the development process; the first step is to identify your message!

THE OVERARCHING RATIONALE: THE ENGAGED CUSTOMER

While your business needs should drive the approach your organization takes to blogging, all business blogs are based on a fundamental premise: the nature of the customer has changed.

We use the term *customer* in the broadest possible sense. You have customers who buy your products or services, certainly, but you have other customers as well. Investors, for example, are customers; they buy shares of stock and hope your company will provide a return on their investment. Partners are customers; they have bought in to the notion that working with you will help them meet their business goals. The media are customers; you hope to sell them on your messages so they can convey those messages to their audiences. Virtually everybody your organization touches is a customer of one kind or another.

A number of timelines come to a climax at the same time, creating a kind of perfect storm with the customer at the apex. These timelines include:

- The long-term, gradual detachment of organizations from their customers
- The increased visibility of business malfeasance, creating a general distrust of businesses and a demand for increased transparency
- The pervasive availability of the Internet coupled with the widespread adoption of high-speed, high-bandwidth access and the development of "social software," including blogs

Let's explore each of these phenomena in a bit more detail.

Organizations Disengage from Customers

In the days before the industrial revolution—before machines—cobblers made shoes. A customer of means who needed a pair of shoes visited a cobbler of choice, who would make shoes fitted to the customer's feet. The customer could request features on his shoes, check on the progress of the shoes as the cobbler worked on them, and then pick them up when they were finished.

Compare that to the relationship between the customer and today's shoe company. The customer walks into a department store or shoe store that carries dozens of separate brands. The customer examines the various styles and picks one she likes. The salesperson, who works for the department store and has limited knowledge about each shoe brand, brings out an already-made pair of those shoes in the size that most closely matches the customer's foot. If the customer wants that design in a slightly different shade of brown, too bad. If she wants a brass buckle instead of a silver one, or a half-inch-shorter heel, the department store salesperson is powerless to help. (Just imagine how flabbergasted the customer would be if the salesperson said, "Hang on, let me call the shoemaker in Italy. I'm sure they can get something right to you.") Once the customer has worn the shoes for a few days, she finds that she has developed a blister on her heel. Again, there's no hope that the manufacturer will do anything about it; she can't even call them. She has to deal with the department store, which may be as many as three or four steps removed from the manufacturer, and even further removed from the craftsman who actually made her pair of shoes.

So, let's review the dilemma in which the customer finds herself:

- She has no input into the style or design of shoes that are available to her.
- She has no connection with the shoemaker through which she might address the shoe's flaws.
- The person with whom she *does* have contact—the department store salesperson—is probably less than enthusiastic about ensuring the customer is thoroughly satisfied with her purchase. After all, *he* didn't make the shoes. And even if he did passionately want to help, there's not a lot he could do.

This simple scenario doesn't begin to address the variety of issues that can arise because of the chasm that has grown between customer and company. The customer cannot talk to others who want the same features in a shoe. The shoemaker is not communicating any issues it is facing, such as a supply problem that led to the temporary use of a second-grade leather which subsequently led to a blister on the customer's heel. And if the customer prefers to do business with companies that espouse certain values, she has to compromise her own values because she has never heard of the company whose name is stamped on the shoebox and she needs those shoes now.

Now, apply the same situation to products and services other than shoes; for instance, cars or software or management consulting services. How about health care? Power tools? Factory equipment?

The inability to influence the products and services available for them to buy, and the perceived lack of interest on the company's part to listen to customers or communicate with them, has created a population of customers whose attitude can be summed up in two words: *fed up*.

Customers Grow Increasingly Skeptical of Organizations

As organizations have grown more distant from their customers, they have also been painted with the brush wielded by those companies that will increase their profits by any means, including those that are unethical and illegal. A spate of business collapses in the late 1990s uncovered business practices that confirmed customers' worst fears. Enron manipulated markets and built a façade of success on a foundation of accounting fraud. The company's failure left thousands of low-level, hard-working employees with no jobs and no retirement nest egg. Shareholders were ruined as their investment was revealed to be worthless. Customers found they had been paying artificially inflated prices.

Enron was only the most visible of the business failures that galvanized lawmakers and other public servants (notably New York Attorney General Elliott Spitzer) to implement severe measures to protect customers against greedy, unethical businesses. The list of businesses that contributed to this perception is a litany of woe: WorldCom, Adelphia, Tyco. While many businesses that are managed to a high ethical standard are suffering unjustly because of the onerous requirements of Sarbanes-Oxley and other rules, there are undoubtedly companies in the marketplace today whose practices are every bit as egregious as those of the companies that have already been caught.

Customers have responded to the deceit and greed of the business world with lower levels of trust. The feeling is that companies do not care what customers want, won't talk to them, and are probably trying to rob them blind and squeeze them for every cent they can get.

Representatives of companies would respond that they *do* communicate. Through press releases riddled with corporate jargon, companies explain their positions, promote their products and services, and tout their value as an investment. They distribute these releases to the media and post them on their companies' Web sites and pat themselves on the back for having communicated so effectively.

Of course, this is decidedly *not* what the fed up, skeptical customer wants. If only there were a vehicle by which customers could engage one another and, perhaps, even engage the company.

Social Software Gives the Customer a Voice

When the Internet first surfaced in the public consciousness in the early 1990s, it was filled with promise. Enthusiasts proclaimed the Net would be the great democratizer, leveling the playing field by empowering the average citizen with the ability to communicate to mass audiences. This vision of the Net was based on two of its most exciting characteristics:

1. *Everybody is a publisher.* Since the first bibles rolled off of Herr Gutenberg's printing press, the ability to publish has remained a privilege of those with the wherewithal to pay for it. Put another way—paraphrasing A.J. Liebling—freedom of the press is a right reserved to those who own one. With the Internet, though, everybody owns one. For the price of basic access, anybody can post a message on a bulletin board or create a Web site.
2. *Everybody is connected to everybody else.* The ability to publish online is of value only because everybody else online can see what you've published. By virtue of a search engine, social connections, or serendipity, other people can find and read what you have written.

Tremendous power rests with these concepts and the first decade of the Net's availability to the general public is rife with examples of individuals bringing that power to bear. Still, it was a very small percentage of the total online population that took advantage of the ability to publish, mainly because while it was available, it wasn't *easy*. Consider the steps necessary to create a Web site:

1. Find a place to host your content.
2. Register a domain name and have the name associated with the space you've acquired on a host's service.
3. Create Web pages in HTML. You must either learn to code in HTML or use a Web-authoring program like Dreamweaver or FrontPage.
4. Transfer your pages from your computer where you created them to your space on the host's server.

Some people found this process fun. Most simply found it overwhelming. They had better things to do than learn a scripting language, find the right FTP software, or figure out how to deal with a domain name service. While they may have yearned for a Web site, the practical implications of actually building and maintaining one presented a significant obstacle.

Then, as though an answer to a prayer, along came blogs and other social software. Social software can be defined as any software that enables the average person to collaborate with others online. Blogs are an example of social software, as are wikis; social tagging sites, such as del.icio.us, http://del.icio.us, and Flickr, http://www.flickr.com; and social networking sites, such as LinkedIn, http://www.linkedin.com. Early examples included instant messaging and message boards, but the new breed of social software is easier to use. The resulting lowered barriers to entry have led to the explosion of blogs, wikis, and social networking sites.

Customers found that blogs were so quick to establish and so easy to use that they began publishing them in droves. By some estimates, 80,000 new blogs are started every day. Customers now have a channel by which they can express their dissatisfaction (or, in many cases, their pleasure) with a company and find other like-minded customers with whom they can share their experiences and plan their responses.

ENGAGING THE CUSTOMER

Customers, fed up with companies that have grown so detached from them, are likely to favor companies that make an effort to close that gap. Companies with blogs—a channel a growing number of customers understand and appreciate—will find themselves attracting customers who are fleeing from competitors that make no effort to re-engage with them.

Consider how a corporate blog might create a dialog with the customer:

- A representative of the company posts a message to a company-sponsored blog addressing some issue of relevance to the organization and of interest to the customer.
- Customers read the post; some contribute comments.
- The employee—along with some of his peers—reads the comments.
- The employee publishes a follow-up post that makes it obvious he has read the customer comments; the current post explains how customer concerns or ideas will be factored into the company's decision.

As a result of this process, customers come away from the blog feeling that they have been heard by real people in the company and that their issues have been taken seriously.

Engaging customers, though, isn't the only reason for a company to pursue a blogging strategy. Other benefits of business blogging include:

- Opening a new marketing channel for products and services
- Reinforcing the company's brand
- Creating a dynamic means for providing customer service and support
- Making company announcements to which people will pay attention

Let's take a look at the various types of business blogs that have emerged over the past couple of years.

Executive Blogs

Blogs by senior company officials—often referred to as CEO blogs, even though most are written by people with titles other than CEO—are among the most common of company blogs. As of this writing, the list of CEO blogs at the Web site The New PR, http://www.thenewpr.com, contains more than 170 blogs by senior executives from around the world. A sampling of these executives includes:

- Paul Woodhouse, CEO of Butler Sheetmetal Ltd in the United Kingdom (blog: Tinbasher)
- Randy Baesler, vice president of marketing, Boeing Commercial Aircraft
- Michael Hyatt, president and CEO, Thomas Nelson Publishers
- Bob Lutz, vice chairman, General Motors
- Jonathan Schwartz, chief technology officer, Sun Microsystems

In these blogs, executives offer their perspectives on issues facing the company. Hearing from the company's leaders—the individuals tasked with the highest-level decision making and planning—can heighten the perception that the company is embracing transparency, a perception enhanced by the reader's ability to comment. Viewed another way, an executive blog eradicates the chasm between customer and company and puts the reader directly in touch with the top dog. Think about the difference between a CEO blog and a CEO's letter to shareholders in an annual report.

Annual Report	Blog
• Appears once a year	• Appears frequently
• Writing is formal	• Writing is candid and authentic
• Covers broad issues	• Focuses on specific issues
• You can't respond to it	• Audience can comment

By way of example, let's look at the blog from Boeing's Baesler. A review of Baesler's recent posts includes the following:

- Seating comfort in the upcoming Boeing 787
- A test flight of a Boeing 737 that includes high-speed Internet connectivity on board
- A reminiscence of the late ABC News anchorman Peter Jennings, who had once toured a Boeing plant

Let's look at one more, the blog from General Motors:

- A piece about strong auto sales and the lack of awareness they have produced
- A post about Lutz delivering the first Pontiac Solstice
- An item about GM's long-term product plans
- A post about plans for the company's performance division

Customers are certainly more likely to want to do business with a company whose leaders are willing to display the kind of leadership qualities embodied by a blog that candidly addresses issues about which customers are interested.

Company Blogs

Who authors an official company blog isn't important, as it is with a CEO blog. In this case, it's just a representative of the company writing on the organization's behalf about goings-on inside the company. In fact, some companies have gone so far as to hire bloggers specifically for this purpose based on their proven ability to write posts in a manner consistent with the expectations of blog-reading customers.

There are plenty of examples of company blogs, including the American Manufacturers Association, which begins its blog, "Welcome to the Manufacturers' blog, one of the top business blogs in the country discussing important issues affecting manufacturing, small businesses, free markets, outsourcing, and staying competitive in the business world."

Technology consulting firm EDS calls its company blog EDS' Next Big Thing Blog. Written by EDS fellows—the elite of the company's technical staff—Next Big Thing looks at the future of technology, something a technology consulting firm should be on top of.

Even the Wharton School at the University of Pennsylvania has a blog dedicated to admissions, covering topics such as the launch of an online MBA application, news about alumni, MBA student activities, and application deadlines.

If these examples sound like items that could be covered on a traditional Web site news page, you're right; they could. Using a blog provides a number of advantages, including speed, the ability for readers to comment, and the presentation of information in a less corporate and more conversational manner.

Not every item, though, would find its way onto a typical corporate news page, however. Consider, for example, a post from the now defunct Daily Scoop from Stonyfield Farm (which was replaced by four more-focused blogs, including the Bovine Bugle, authored by the same individual):

Forget the Scope & TicTacs, pass the yogurt

At a big important convention this week—the International Association for Dental Research—researchers outlined the results of a study that seemed to indicate that eating yogurt could do away with halitosis, the dreaded bad breath.

Hurrah! While we here at Stonyfield are always on the lookout for all the good things yogurt can do for you, this one took us by surprise. Maybe we'll start producing a minty-fresh version. What do you think?

Okay, the study only included 24 people who ate 6 ounces of yogurt a day—(to which we say, "Hey, that's not nearly enough! We eat 6 ounces before breakfast!")—for six weeks. In the end, they were shown to have lower levels of odor-causing compounds, such as hydrogen sulfide, in their mouths.

The study results suggest that the active bacteria in yogurt, specifically Streptococcus thermophilus and Lactobacillus bulgaricus, may have a beneficial effect on odor-causing bacteria in the mouth. (We have four more beneficial bacterias in our yogurts, but we won't get into that here.)

The study participants also had lower levels of plaque and the gum disease gingivitis. Now that's interesting.

We're not ready to make these claims just yet, but if you're interested, you can read up on all the good cultures in our yogurts here.

This post is instructive! Note the conversational tone, which makes you feel that the writer (a writer named Christine Halvorson hired as chief blogger) is speaking to you. The style is more engaging, leading more people to want to read. What corporate press release would use phrases like "a big important convention," "hurrah!," and "Hey, that's not nearly enough!"? While most organizations have a hard time getting anybody to pay attention to their news, Halvorson's personable approach has led many to subscribe via RSS just so they can stay current with her latest observations.

Product Blogs

Organizations can take a couple approaches to product blogs. One approach is to provide updates about the product so customers can stay up to date on issues affecting their purchases. Another targets fans of a product, providing them with insights and information directly from those who are responsible for their favorite brands.

A product blog that keeps customers current can build greater loyalty to the product and the company that makes it. Consider The Official QuickBooks Online Weblog. Quickbooks Online is the Web-based version of Intuit's business accounting software and the blog is written by members of the product team. A sampling of posts includes information about browser security (because the tool is accessed over the Web), an answer to a customer question about why the software version number that displays in the URL is constantly changing, and another answer to a customer question about how to back up online data. Addressing customer questions on a blog makes a lot of sense, because you don't know how many other customers may have the same question. The blog also is used to announce promotions and offer tips on using the software. Compare this to competitive products that have no blog, leaving customers detached from the organization. This approach sends the message, "You bought our product and now we'll have nothing to do with you unless you call us" while the blog approach says, "You bought our product and now you're part of our community. Let's stay in touch."

The General Motors Smallblock Engine blog, which was retired after one year, provided an example of a blog for fans of a product. Unlike the company's FastLane blog, which addresses issues around cars for car buyers in order to create a community and establish a dialogue, the Smallblock Engine blog—launched on a significant product anniversary—was aimed at hardcore fans of the engine. On April 12, 2005, GM Powertrain Group Vice President Tom Stephens posted this missive: "As you know, we will launch the new LS7 engine in the 2006 Corvette Z06 this summer. The LS7 will be the first engine to bear the 'SAE Power and Torque Certified' label, and General Motors has become the first manufacturer to certify an engine's horsepower and torque rating under the new Society of Automotive Engineers J2723 test procedure. We're proud to be the first to certify an engine and pleased with the LS7 results. We have four other engines going through certification now, and others will follow, as we want customers to have accurate information when they make a purchase decision. We encourage all manufacturers to do the same."

Here's a typical comment that resulted from the post: "Great news on the certification results. Congratulations! Now I must ask when this engine will be mated to a 6-speed paddle shift transmission in the Z06 or will GM determinedly shoot itself in the foot by continuing to ignore the reality that that type of transmission sells noticeably well when offered?" Clearly, this is a fan of the product with a strong interest in how it will be presented. The blog provides such fans with the opportunity to engage those who influence the product's direction.

Customer Service Blogs

Similar to product blogs, customer service blogs focus exclusively on issues a product is facing so customers are always aware of problems and company plans to address them. eBay maintains such a blog for its developer's network, providing updates and resources that are useful (and sometimes downright important) to developers. A review of the blog as of this writing reveals policy changes, the availability of new software, new documentation eBay made available, and the introduction of a new service.

Advocacy Blogs

Some organizations advocate around specific issues. A blog dedicated to an issue provides interested audiences with updates on the company's actions, positions, and reactions to developments. AARP—the association representing senior citizens in the United States—maintains such a blog focusing on government plans to overhaul the Social Security system, a subject of intense interest to AARP members, many of whom rely on their Social Security payments.

Another example comes from Cisco Systems, which maintains a blog on its government relations efforts.

Employee Blogs

Official company blogs by any employee who wants to write one represent the most perplexing category of blogs for most organizations. Company lawyers, in particular, worry about what an employee might say in a blog about work, particularly when that blog is not subject to review and approval. (We'll look more closely at this issue in Chapters 3 and 12 where we'll talk about employee blogging and legal issues. The short answer, though, is that a well-communicated employee blogging policy should address any concerns.)

More important is the question of why a company would want to let employees blog about the company and their jobs. Those fed-up customers who are sick of dealing with interactive voice response systems as their only means of engaging the company will be thrilled to hear the voices of real employees, speaking in their own human voices, and to tap into these resources when they need to interact with the organization.

There are, of course, even more reasons to let employees blog. Michael Hyatt, the CEO of Thomas Nelson Publishers, articulated three reasons he wanted his employees to start blogging about work:

1. To raise the visibility of our company and our products
2. To make a contribution to the publishing community
3. To give people a look at what goes on inside a real publishing company

IBM is actively encouraging its nearly 300,000 employees to blog on the company's behalf. You can find a list of Sun Microsystems employee bloggers, of which there are hundreds. Robert Scoble, whose blog is referenced in Chapter 1, is one of several hundred Microsoft bloggers who blog about work and about the company.

Microsoft provides an excellent example of the benefit a company can accrue from letting employees blog. In some circles, Microsoft has had a reputation for arrogance, accused of releasing software that should still be in a beta test phase and forcing the public to put up with bugs, security flaws, and a host of other problems. People who viewed Microsoft this way saw its culture set by the richest man in the world. Today, however, vast numbers of customers and others see Microsoft as a company populated by real people—like Scoble—who do real work and are passionate about it. It's clear from reading Microsoft employee blogs that these employees care about the work they do, they're dedicated to providing customers with the best possible product, and they're more than willing to listen when the public has a problem. This new connection genuine employees have established with the company has begun to have a real impact on the public's view of the company.

Blogs in a Crisis

A company's reputation is never at greater risk than when a crisis strikes. In fact, the definition of a corporate crisis is an unexpected event or revelation that threatens the company's reputation. A lot of so-called experts have proclaimed blogs a must-have tool during a crisis. By now, the benefits of a blog during a crisis should be obvious, including the ability to provide timely updates and for the company to address the situation in an authentic, human voice.

However, there aren't many ideas worse than launching a blog at the time of a crisis. Without established goodwill among readers, the blog could deteriorate quickly into a venue for critics to assail the organization. A new blog doesn't even have to be focused on a crisis to have this deleterious effect. A blog started by Paul Purdue, CEO if iFulfill (an e-commerce order fulfillment business) focused on lighter issues, but Purdue started the blog as the company was in the stages of failing. The comment tool was used for unhappy customers to vent about their problems.

Conversely, a blog that has existed for a while and built goodwill among its readers can serve a company mightily when a crisis hits. That was the case with BigHa, the Oregon-based company that produces (among other things) the powerful laser lights that a New Jersey man used to point at aircraft landing at New York's

Kennedy International Airport. BigHa, a company that had managed to conduct business beneath the radar of the press, was suddenly in the spotlight, accused of producing weapons of terrorism. (The lasers were in fact manufactured primarily for amateur astronomers to point to constellations.)

BigHa sales and marketing executive Noah Acres had blogged on behalf of the company for some time when the crisis hit. He already had an audience of readers who appreciated his input. When he began posting items about the crisis, he had the sympathy of his readers, who provided an alternative viewpoint to that expressed by many in the mainstream media. Acres was even able to respond to media statements in the blog.

SUMMARY

Blogging, as *Business Week* noted in its May 2, 2005, edition, is here to stay as a business consideration, both from the standpoint of monitoring blogs and producing your own. You can use blogs

- for company leaders to communicate with customers,
- for employees to communicate with customers,
- to reinforce your brand,
- to produce organizational transparency,
- to keep customers updated on product issues,
- to serve as a channel to the public in a crisis, and
- to report to a constituent audience on the company's positions.

There is one other business use of a blog that we'll address in the next chapter: blogging to employees over the company's intranet.

3

BLOGS ON THE INSIDE

Blogs can be every bit as powerful *inside* the organization as they can outside, and in many instances even more so. Mounted on an intranet and made available to employees, blogs can serve as one of the most effective knowledge-sharing tools a company can implement. They can establish an institutional memory where none existed before and open a dialogue between leaders and employees that informs decision making and heightens employee engagement. Blogs can transform a static, one-way, top-down intranet into a dynamic, interactive collaboration tool that can be felt directly on the company's bottom line.

An intranet is similar to the Internet captured within an organization. Based primarily on Web content—that is, content coded in HTML and displayed on a Web browser—intranets provide lightning-quick access to information (such as policies and other documentation), communicate news, and host transactions (such as benefits enrollments, performance evaluations, budgeting, submitting expense reports, and a broad range of other processes that used to require the completion of a paper form). In addition to the internal Web (sometimes referred to as the corporate web), intranets also are comprised of e-mail, file transfer, and all the other components of TCP/IP–Transmission Control Protocol/ Internet Protocol–the suite of rules that lets computers talk to one another and empower the Internet.

Blogs are a perfect tool for intranets and are already being applied in companies ranging from high-tech (such as Intel, IBM, Microsoft, and Sun Microsystems) to manufacturing-based companies (such as Siemens USA) to a broad range of other types of organizations (such as The Walt Disney Company). Compared to knowledge management databases that can cost hundreds of thousands of dollars—and more—blogs can be implemented at little or no cost. And, unlike those same expensive knowledge management databases, blogs are intuitive to most employees. Their potential to improve productivity, time-to-market, employee turnover, and a host of other measures that tend to keep management awake at night is unmatched by any online technology since the introduction of the intranet itself.

THE ONE REQUIREMENT: EMPLOYEES AS PUBLISHERS

The biggest obstacle organizations face in tapping into blogs' potential on intranets is resistance to the idea that any employee can publish. In far too many organizations, the intranet is viewed as a closed system to which only authorized contributors may provide information.

Certainly, the production of much content on a company's intranet should be limited to authorized personnel. You wouldn't want just any employee editing the company's employment policy or amending its medical benefit plans. This official content can be clearly distinguished from employee-generated content.

(Consumer-generated media on the Web is known as CGM, so we'll refer to employee-generated media as EGM.) Many organizations have implemented message boards as a knowledge management tool; this is content that isn't produced by anybody in any kind of official capacity. Blogs are no different, and can be clearly labeled as EGM just so nobody gets confused.

There are still many organizations that reject even message boards, though. Management views message boards as an activity distinct from work, or a productivity drain, or they worry employees will write unflattering comments about them. In fact, message boards, applied properly, allow employees who might otherwise never find each other to share information and knowledge needed to make the best decisions or just to get the job done.

Blogs represent a new option for this kind of knowledge transfer. Employees who opt to create internal blogs can keep co-workers apprised of what they're up to or what progress they've made on a given task or project. They can share information they've found that others could find useful, making that information discoverable through an intranet search. More to the point, though, is that employee blogs on an intranet would function just like blogs on the Web. Employees would link to those colleagues' blogs that help them do their jobs better or faster. They would get to know which blogs most often provide valuable content and include them on their blogrolls, making them more easily accessible to others exploring this internal blogosphere. It can actually be dizzying to think about how freely knowledge would fly through an organization in a well-managed blogspace.

There are some organizations that have dismissed internal blogs because, they say, they already host message boards. Aren't they the same? In fact, they are quite distinct. While they both are built for conversation, a message board promotes free-wheeling discussions that anybody can initiate. Blogs, on the other hand, place the locus of control (as it is described by blogger Lee LeFevre on his blog, Common Craft) squarely with the blog's author(s). The personality of the blogger dominates the voice of the blog.

Blogs lend themselves to several internal uses in organizations enlightened enough to support employee blogging. These include the general categories detailed below.

Project blogs. Projects suffer a unique fate in companies everywhere. After completion, all the learnings the project produced are slowly lost to time. Anybody undertaking a similar project a year or two later is likely to make the same mistakes, struggle to find information a previous project had already uncovered, and encounter the same obstacles. When it comes to projects, most organizations have no institutional memory.

Fortunately, blogs are here to save the day. There are two approaches to blogging to support the success of projects:

1. *Project journal.* In this case, a project manager maintains a daily journal recounting progress for the day. Some projects won't require daily postings, in which case only major points on the project's timeline prompt a posting. These points include information needed and information found, milestones reached, obstacles encountered and how they were overcome, and goals achieved.

   In addition to becoming a permanent record, a project blog serves the information needs of other employees who have a stake in the project. And employees who read the blog can provide solutions to problems, respond to calls for information, and help the team overcome obstacles.

2. *Project team blog.* Members of the project team should have a blog where they share information with one another. By posting to a blog—especially when assigning each post to a project-relevant category—team members are able to engage in an ongoing conversation about the project even when

they aren't in the same room, the same building, or even the same time zone.

News blogs. Work is social. After all, what is the definition of an organization if not a group of people who come together in order to achieve common goals? Whenever you put a group of people together, you have a social environment. You can resist it or you can take advantage of it.

People are naturally interested in other people. This is why the dreaded four B's have been a staple of internal communications since companies began communicating. You don't know the dreaded four B's? They are:

1. Birthdays
2. Brides
3. Babies
4. Bowling scores

In other words, all those personnel-related notices that also can include service anniversaries, retirements, obituaries, and a host of other items. Since time immemorial, employee communications professionals have labored to produce these items when they could have been focusing on strategic communication designed to advance the company's agenda.

With blogs, employees can produce this information themselves. Blogs can be assigned based on business unit, geographic location, or any other way you might slice or dice your organization.

Facility blogs can also allow employees to post local news, such as achievement of a workplace safety goal, an upcoming barbecue or holiday party, pavement resurfacing work in the parking lot, and lost rings recovered from rest rooms.

Customer and competitor blogs. Most employees are not in direct contact with customers. Yet every employee should be working to satisfy customers. The farther removed you are from the customer, though, the less you know about his likes and dislikes, pet peeves, genuine needs, preferences, opinions, and quirks.

In fact, knowing the customer is a crucial element of workplace literacy—one that most employees are woefully lacking. Using a customer blog, those employees who *do* work one-on-one with customers can post insights that would help other employees gear their efforts toward addressing the issues raised.

Knowledge of the competition is another aspect of workplace literacy that drives employee engagement. A blog about the company's competitors—even blogs dedicated to single competitors, if they're big enough, important enough, or threatening enough— will help employees make sure their efforts are helping exploit competitors' weaknesses or bolster the company's strengths.

Cross-functional team blogs. Teams whose membership crosses organizational boundaries are ripe for blogs. These are employees who, unlike members of the same department, do not see each other every day or communicate on the familiar basis of teams that work together routinely. Yet they are working together on common goals or sharing a common subject matter expertise. Consider, for example, these kinds of teams:

- *Web developers.* This includes anybody in the company who works on Web-based content production, design, or management, including the external Web, the intranet, and any extranets the company may maintain.
- *Subject matter experts.* In most large organizations, corporate HR is only one part of the picture; each business unit has its own HR staff. A blog could allow these individuals to share knowledge around issues such as recruiting or compensation. Another example: Many companies employ regulatory affairs experts in each business unit. Using a blog,

these professionals could offer their insights and experiences to others who practice the same skills.

- *Ad hoc teams.* Any team that comes together to achieve short-term goals would benefit from a blog.
- *Standing teams.* Employee recreation teams, quality improvement teams, and a host of other cross-functional teams are common in any number of companies. Again, blogs serve as an ideal tool for allowing team members to share knowledge and information and stay current on the team's activities.

Individual employee blogs. This is the class of intranet blogs that most concerns management in a lot of organizations, yet those organizations that have employed them are experiencing far more benefits than problems. Microsoft and IBM, for example, are finding employee blogs can speed the transfer of knowledge through the organization faster than a sinister virus can sweep through the Internet.

Ensuring employee blogs remain focused on business and work is a simple matter of articulating and communicating an internal blogging policy. Insisting that internal blogs be used primarily for work-related purposes, though, does not mean they shouldn't be fun or that employees could never post anything other than work-related posts.

Remember: Work is social. While companies may spend jaw-dropping amounts of money on knowledge databases, these databases are capable of storing only structured data. The vast majority of knowledge and information in an organization is unstructured, swimming around in the heads of your employees. That's right; most of the knowledge in your company goes home every night!

Consequently, knowledge is best transferred person-to-person, not computer-to-person. Yet the computer can serve as a very efficient delivery channel for employee A to transfer information from his head to the head of employee B. This social form of knowledge transfer often happens serendipitously. At the pharmaceutical company Allergan, the research and development building's walls are all made of dry-mark erase board so two scientists who happen to meet in the hall and strike up a conversation can, if inspiration strikes, begin diagramming then and there. There's more than one company where the best knowledge transfer occurs outside among the smokers. Think about it: A bunch of employees from different departments with nothing in common but work. What do you suppose they talk about?

Blogs can bring this model of knowledge transfer to all employees and strengthen it through links and blogrolls, search results, and building of blog communities. And what does it matter if an employee occasionally posts an item about his kids, her hobby, his favorite sports team, her MBA class? Other employees interested in the subject will gravitate to these blogs, learning in the process about the employee who wrote it, and what the employee does and knows, filing that source of information away until it's needed to complete a task or solve a problem.

At Siemens USA, management allows such posts, unconcerned about what others may lament as lost work time, as long as employee bloggers also get their work done on time. And in companies where employees are permitted to blog, most posts do indeed share useful knowledge.

Department blogs. Not all blogs need to be free-flowing conversations penned by random employees. Department blogs come in two flavors, one community generated and the other authored by the department manager.

The department manager's blog is her opportunity to keep members of the team up to date on everything they need to know. For example, she could provide updates on her meetings with her boss (so employees know what her higher-ups expect of her), keep teams advised of the progress of other departmental teams, post reminders, let employees know of shifting priorities and shine the spotlight on employees who have earned departmental recognition.

Much of this is currently communicated haphazardly in organizations, at staff meetings, for instance, or informally. Because blog posts don't need to be long and formal (the way memos are written), it becomes a very quick task for the manager to crank out these updates—sometimes as short as a sentence or two.

The employee-generated departmental blog is simply a place for employees to post information they think other members of the same department would find interesting or useful. Creating meaningful categories makes it easy for employees to stay on top of just the information that's pertinent to them, although if they get departmental blog posts in their news readers, they will need only a few seconds to scan headlines and determine what's important anyway.

One additional departmental blog to consider is the outward-facing blog—one designed to inform employees from *outside* the department of news and information they may need to know. The information technology department provides a great example. Have you ever received an e-mail message letting you know that the product sales database server will go down for an upgrade at 1:00 AM on Saturday morning and that it should be back online by 5:00 AM Monday morning? Why can't IT just post that information to a blog? Those interested in knowing such things can subscribe to the feed; those who aren't never have to be bothered about it again.

CEO blogs. In those days of distant memory before intranets, untold numbers of companies communicated with employees by publishing company magazines and newsletters. A column from the CEO or president was among the most standard of features in these publications, usually appearing on the inside front cover or just after the table of contents. They were rarely actually written by the CEO or president, who would convey to a staff writer what he wanted to get across to employees each month. Because the publication was distributed weeks after the column was written, and because it went to every employee, the column tended to be fairly generic: "I'm counting on every employee to renew his or her commitment to customer satisfaction, which is increasingly important in our low-margin, highly competitive environment." Or worse, "We need to leverage our core competencies in support of our goal of achieving world class status as we shift our paradigms and focus on mission-critical tasks."

How much better and more relevant would a blog be if written by the CEO whenever he had something on his mind? An apt title for every intranet's CEO blog could be What Kept Me Awake Last Night. As we've noted so often, the best blog posts are often the shortest, so we're not talking about a time-consuming chore for the CEO. But consider the payoff!

A study of 40,000 employees conducted by the human resources consulting firm Towers Perrin determined that the most crucial factor in motivating employees to apply their best, most determined efforts to the company's success is the belief that the company's senior leaders have employees' interests at heart. The study—and others that support this finding—makes it clear that employees want to hear from the source that the company's leaders are making the right decisions to support the company's growth and success.

If this sounds a lot like employees need to trust senior management, you're right. Study after study confirms that trust is the single most important factor driving employee commitment and job satisfaction. Employees also want to be involved; employee involvement is a major factor in building commitment to the organization's goals and objectives, according to research.

Now consider how a CEO or president's blog would work. The big cheese publishes a post that reads something like this: "In an executive committee meeting yesterday, we spent some time talking about ways to fend off a challenge from our key competitor. Some of the ideas raised include A, B, and C. I have to believe there are other options available, and I'm anxious to hear what those of you who deal with these issues every day have to suggest. But if you think the ideas I listed above are good ones, please let me know that, too." And the comments come flooding in from employees delighted that the top dog is asking directly for their help.

Or the president uses the blog to explain a decision, allowing employees to explain how they feel about it. Any concerns that employees will abuse the privilege and mouth off inappropriately to the president evaporate when you realize all comments must be signed. This doesn't mean employees can't voice disagreement with the decision. The ability to post negative comments—while unwanted by some leaders—sends the message to the entire workforce that their opinions are respected, building trust and fueling the growth of the highly engaged population.

It's not an unheard-of concept, by the way. Intel's president, Paul Otellini, writes an intranet blog, for example.

Business unit leader blogs. The cascade model of employee communication is sound in principle. The idea is actually pretty simple. The company's senior leaders articulate an idea in the broadest terms. Business unit leaders interpret that message to explain what it means to employees in that business unit. Managers, in turn, explain what it means to workers in their departments. And team leaders tell employees what it means in their day-to-day efforts.

Unfortunately, the cascade approach rarely works. There are too many opportunities for the message to be garbled, miscommunicated, or not communicated at all. A blog can go a long way toward solving the problem, because now all managers have access to the same translation as posted by the business unit leader, and the ability to post questions or observations that can help both managers and the business unit leader better understand and execute the plan.

Corporate news blogs. Important, sensitive, and serious news should be communicated seriously. Good employee communication writers know how to use the best elements of style guides like those from AP and the *New York Times* to ensure the gravity of the news is clear.

Not all news is all that important, sensitive, or serious.

At Siemens USA, second-tier news is communicated through a blog. The manager of employee communications writes the blog under her byline. The more conversational approach to this news engages employees, who often post comments. For example, when the National Geographic Society used Siemens equipment to produce a startling image of King Tut's mummy, manager Shelley Brown wrote about it on the news blog. Responses from employees focused mainly on pride in seeing their equipment used in so intriguing a manner.

The blog was named in a "name-the-blog" contest that prompted submissions from hundreds of employees. The winning entry was Blogger von Siemens, a send-up of the founder's name, Frederick von Siemens. Blogger von Siemens appears on the intranet's home page, just below the serious headlines.

WEB FEEDS IN THE WORKPLACE

Just as the global blogging phenomenon was driven by the idea of Web feeds (RSS and Atom), these feeds can help employees focus their attention on information that is important and stay current without having to visit every intranet blog that contains useful content.

And, just as on the Web, while blogs generate feeds automatically, you don't need a blog to support a feed.

The idea that underlies the news reader (or news aggregator) is all about attention. While it is impossible for the average employee to make a daily visit to every intranet page that may contain useful information, it takes only a couple of minutes to read through the feeds of each of those pages using software that aggregates the content all in one place. Further, employees who read external blogs about their field of work aggregate them in the same place.

Intranet web pages that can be feed enabled but don't necessarily need to take the form of a blog include the following:

- IT updates (like planned server downtime)
- Homepage news items
- Health and safety reports
- Financial performance releases
- Press releases issued publicly

Offering feeds will probably require some kind of education. A solution is to build a feed landing page that explains what they are and how they work, and provides a list of links to all the company's available feeds, instructions for setting up feeds, and downloads of feed newsreaders. If you don't want to have every employee install newsreader software on their computers, the company could build a Web-based newsreader, similar to Bloglines, NewsGator Online, and NewsIsFree on the World Wide Web.

SUMMARY

In many ways, blogs can produce even greater return on investment when applied internally than they can on the World Wide Web. Intranet blogs oil the machinery of knowledge transfer and provide the foundation for institutional memory. To take advantage of intranet blogs, though, senior leaders need to understand the benefits the organization can accrue when employees can self-publish to the intranet, a significant change from the authorized-publishers-only approach most companies take to their intranets.

Now that we've explored the ideas behind blogs, it's time to get down and dirty with details on how to effectively monitor the blogosphere.

4

MONITORING
THE BLOGOSPHERE

Most organizations care about what the media says about them, as well as what the media says about their industry and their competitors. Negative media attention can be extremely damaging, even leading to decreased revenue, market share, morale, and employee retention. Organizations often have staff or entire departments focused on getting positive media attention.

Media monitoring can reveal what is being said about your executives, your organization, your industry, and your competitors. Most organizations monitor the media, and today that needs to include blogs. Not monitoring blogs will put your organization at a disadvantage; any serious competition is or will be soon monitoring, and you had better have access to the same information sources, namely blogs.

Often important news is reported in blogs before the mainstream media and at times only reported in blogs. Bloggers are usually subject matter experts about the topics on which they blog, unlike mainstream media journalists who are often generalists. Sometimes bloggers may be the only ones who get it right, and oftentimes only people in that particular field care about the subject. If it's your field or industry that's involved, reading relevant blogs is critical.

Another reason to monitor blogs is to know what your peers, competitors, customers, and other important people are saying. The number of people blogging and the amount of information in the blogosphere is increasing rapidly; chances are if your competitors or customers are not blogging yet, they may be soon.

Monitoring blogs can assess buzz around an organization, and its issues, products, and services. What the blogosphere is saying should inform a company's marketing and communications groups of the buzz, and could even lead to an adjustment, particularly if the blogosphere has picked up on a feature or aspect of a product/service that suggests to the company that it should shine a spotlight on this feature or aspect in its traditional marketing.

Monitoring also helps an organization determine when it should contact somebody directly. When Dan Entin wrote in his blog Two Percent Nation that he couldn't find his favorite deodorant, Degree Sport Solid, the company that manufactures it, Unilever, shipped him a case and sent him a list of local stores that carried it. He wrote about it and Unilever received tremendous buzz. You can't buy publicity like that! Other companies, for example Land Rover and Dell, have received negative buzz in the blogosphere and these cases suggest monitoring would have revealed these attacks on the companies' reputations early and allowed the companies to address them quickly.

RESPONDING TO NEGATIVE STATEMENTS, INACCURACIES, MISINFORMATION, AND ATTACKS

Honesty is a wonderful thing, and on the Internet and especially blogs, it is essential. It's hard to lie or exaggerate when just about anyone in entire world can stop by at any time and read what you're saying. The whole world can correct you if you're lying—*someone* will know. Even if comments are not enabled on your blog, people will comment on their own blogs. Other people will link and comment on other people's posts, and soon the whole world will know you're lying. If you're really stupid and dishonest about it, heads will probably roll.

You certainly don't need a blog for a blogger to attack you. If the attack resonates, it takes only a day or two for word to spread. An intense negative *blog swarm,* as it is sometimes called, can do immense damage. A blog swarm is when many blogs, perhaps even thousands, start posting negative material on a subject and feed off of each other's energy, commenting on each other's opinions and facts that are discovered.

Negative blog storms have been responsible for damage to ex-Senate Republican Leader Trent Lott, CBS News' ex-anchorman Dan Rather, CNN's ex-news director Eason Jordan, and the *New York Times* ex-editor Howell Raines. In particular, they are responsible for the "ex" part of those men's titles. The details are in the blogosphere and easily looked up.

There is a growing number of cautionary tales of the consequences of a blog swarm. CBS News' "Rathergate" fiasco is one. CBS had obtained some potentially damaging yet fake documents pertaining to U.S. President George Bush. It continued to defend the documents blindly despite increasingly overwhelming evidence from the blogosphere that the documents were false. The damage to its brand was significant and its viewership significantly smaller in its aftermath.

On the business side, consider the story of Kryptonite, a company that makes high-end bicycle locks. A bicyclist figured out how to pick the locks with the back end of a Bic pen and posted his discovery to a bicycling message board. It was read by a blogger who posted the lock hack to his blog. Other bloggers read the item and posted their own items linking back to the original blogger's post. Soon, another blogger shot a video of himself picking the lock. This was picked up by Engadget, one of the A-list blogs read by hundreds of thousands of people. The story found its way into the mainstream press within a day of Engadget's post.

If intense negative comments start to surface, they need to be dealt with swiftly and honestly. The luxury of at least a *little* time to which organizations are accustomed does not exist in the blogosphere. Denying accusations categorically and insulting bloggers is exactly what CBS did, and it obviously doesn't work. Kryptonite continued to assess the situation and strategize a response, while the situation got more and more out of hand every day they waited. Transparency and honesty will minimize damage. Admit mistakes—you will *not* be able to hide them.

This does not mean, however, that you need to respond to each and every item that swarms through the blogosphere. Each instance warrants its own analysis in order to arrive at the best judgment. For example, consider the case of retailer Target, the focus of some blog swarming. The company never responded, and in this instance, not responding was the right approach to take.

Amazon.com provides the infrastructure for Target's online store via its Web Services offering. The store sold many books online, but they didn't display in the Target design the same way they did on Amazon's site. A search for the word "marijuana" on Target's site revealed text that read:

Marijuana
$25.25

Of course, Target wasn't selling pot. It was the title of a book, but the way the information—all pulled from a database—appeared on the page did not make this clear. A screen shot of the page quickly made its way through the blogosphere, and Steve Rubel— the A-list PR blogger—called it a PR crisis.

But the mainstream media never picked up on the story and it just as quickly vanished from the radar screen. The reason: Absolutely nobody thought Target was *actually* selling marijuana. The authorities didn't raid the place and stoners didn't place their orders. Something else was clearly the cause of this error, so nobody got too worked up. Ultimately, a few bloggers figured out what the truth was by finding the book on Amazon.com, and they posted their findings.

Target, for its part, remained silent. Not a word about the issue was uttered by its PR staff or other representatives. Their judgment appears to have been right; there was no need to respond.

When you *do* respond, you also have to figure out what form that response will take. In most instances when you are under assault, there is nothing to be gained by engaging in the discussion and subjecting yourself to immediate attacks. It is best to use more traditional channels. The recent case of the Apple iPod Nano illustrates the wisdom of this approach.

In September 2005, Apple CEO Steve Jobs stunned the marketplace with the introduction of the Nano, an ultra-small, ultra-thin version of Apple's wildly successful digital media player. The Nano was in instant high demand and began flying off store shelves. It didn't take long, though, before reports started circulating through the blogosphere that the Nano screen was easily scratched and the damage so severe that it was impossible to view information or artwork displayed on the screen.

One dissatisfied customer created a Web site, http://www.flawedmusicplayer.com. He received more than 30 e-mails per hour at one point, many with photos of people's damaged iPods. Blogs of all kinds reported on the issue; a search on Feedster using the keywords "Nano" and "scratches" produced over 3,100 posts!

Apple took about four days before responding, which it did through normal media contact. A press release generated interviews between reporters and Apple spokespersons. The mainstream media covered the announcement that Apple believed only about one-tenth of 1 percent of all the Nanos made were affected, and that those who had bought a defective Nano would get a replacement. Matthew Peterson, who created the complaint site, removed all the content, replacing it with the headline, "Apple does the right thing." In his introduction to the replacement narrative, Peterson wrote, "For me personally this issue is over. I took down the Web site of my own accord. I started the site to get Apple's attention. Mission accomplished. Now that they have investigated what my site was alleging, and made their own statement and rectified the situation to my (and everyone who has a broken Nano screen) satisfaction, I have chosen to take down my site. Please do not ask me for pictures or e-mails from people with the problem. As this issue is resolved, I don't think any of this information is relevant to anyone. I never started out to bash Apple and I am going to keep my integrity on that by removing the site and thanking Apple for looking into this and replacing the screens of those people who have been unfortunate to receive one of the 'vendor problem' screens."

The issue, then, spread through the blogosphere, but Apple never had to use the blogosphere to address it. (Which is a good thing, because Apple doesn't have a corporate blog.)

If your company *does* have its own blog, you can use it to address an attack, as Oregon-based BigHa did (as described in Chapter 2).

And, of course, if the attack is malicious and unjustified, you have the option of turning to your lawyers. The case would have to be particularly egregious to warrant this extreme, no matter how much you might want to sue somebody who attacks you or posts inaccurate information about you. Let's look at the reactions to the way two companies handled a similar situation.

When two blogs dedicated to Apple's Macintosh computer posted leaked information about products in development, Apple responded by suing the bloggers—one of them a 19-year-old college student—to reveal the names of the Apple employees who had leaked the information. Apple is a popular company among bloggers but was nevertheless vilified for its action, which was condemned by the Electronic Frontier Foundation, a lobbying group that provided pro bono counsel to the bloggers.

Sun Microsystems also experienced leaks by employees. At Sun, the problem was handled entirely differently. Its chief technology officer, Jonathan Schwartz—also the company's highest-ranked blogger—posted an appeal to employees on his blog. "For the sake of your colleagues around Sun, please do not share Sun's confidential information. There have been a few instances in recent weeks where crucial data and photos were leaked from Sun. It probably sounds counterintuitive, but this actually harms Sun's business," Schwartz wrote. He added (in addition to other commentary), "As you know, I'm a huge believer in 'opening' Sun to the world—that's what this blogs.sun.com infrastructure is all about—transparency is one our best competitive weapons. But the unauthorized sharing of Sun confidential information is illegal, and against company policy."

This was a remarkable approach to the issue. In a display of complete transparency, Schwartz posted the note to his *public* blog, knowing it was widely read by employees. Schwartz and Sun came off looking enlightened and employees got the message to knock off the leaks. This was a far better approach than Apple's.

OTHERS WILL MONITOR YOUR BLOGS

It is also important to realize that competitors, customers, and others can monitor anything you or your company say. Although it is possible to have a "private" blog, one behind a firewall or with other limited access, most blogs are extremely public. When the public nature of blogs is combined with their informal writing style, occasionally "slips" are made. These can be broken down into two types of mistakes: ones where inappropriate company information is released and ones where inappropriate personal topics are discussed or inappropriate personal information is publicized.

A company-specific mistake is made when a blogger releases information that is not supposed to be public information. This might be upcoming product plans, internal financial numbers, customer-specific information, or just about anything else. Bloggers need guidelines about what company information is appropriate to blog about, and more companies are releasing blogging policies that encompass appropriate company-specific guidelines.

An equally or maybe even more common problem is when bloggers blog on inappropriate topics or release inappropriate personal information. This can be either in a personal blog or on company blogs. There needs to be guidelines (i.e., a blogging policy) as well as an application of common sense. Bloggers have been fired for what companies considered inappropriate blogging, including some very high-profile cases. Employees have been fired for information in their own personal blogs, including a flight attendant for a major airline who wore her uniform in some photos the airline deemed inappropriate, and a new employee for a search engine company who blogged about a company event where apparently an excess of alcohol was consumed. We discuss blogging policies and the legal aspects of blogging in Chapter 12.

People often are nastier and meaner in e-mail than in person. Many a mild-mannered person occasionally releases surprisingly vitriolic e-mails, often entirely out of character. Blogs sometimes seem to raise this to an even higher and more inappropriate level. Bloggers regularly release details of their personal lives they wouldn't tell their closest friend, refer to their boss by entirely inappropriate names, and say things they would never say in public. There needs to be a comprehensive and understandable blogging policy, an application of common sense, a realization that blogs are public, and a distinction between public and private lives.

Even if a blogger has an anonymous blog, releasing too many personal details can render that blog no longer anonymous. Spouses and bosses can realize they are being described (usually in less-than-flattering terms) and respond in undesired ways. More than one "anonymous" blogger has been fired for totally inappropriate and self-identifying comments.

SEARCH ENGINES

Search engines are extremely useful in monitoring what is being said in blogs. Several types of search engines exist, including general purpose search engines, blog-specific search engines, and RSS search engines. It is important to realize that no search engine is perfect and it's necessary to use more than one. A search on Google versus one on Yahoo!, both general purpose search engines, will differ dramatically in both what they return and the order of what they return. The first page results on the major search engines show surprisingly little overlap. A search using Daypop, a current events search engine, will typically return more timely information but will search significantly fewer sources. A search with Technorati, which searches only blogs, will return yet a different set of results. Don't expect any of these searches to be exhaustive, even for the type of sources in which they specialize. They can and will miss information at times, which necessitates using multiple search engines.

General Purpose Search Engines

The most popular search engines are Google, Yahoo!, and MSN, according to Nielsen//NetRatings. Together they comprise the large majority of Web searches. They index billions of pages each. Yahoo! is currently claiming 19.2 billion pages. Searching for your company name, executives' names, and trademarks can reveal surprising information at times and is something that should be done regularly. Google Alerts will even periodically e-mail you when new occurrences of any search terms you specify are found. Google Alerts can search news, the Web, both, or groups. News Alerts are generated when a search term is found in the top ten results of a Google News search, Web Alerts are generated when a search term is found in the top 20 results of a Google Web search, and Group Alerts are generated when a search term is found in the top 50 results of a Google Group search.

The following is a Google Alert result delivered via e-mail for "Ted Demopoulos":

> Google Alert for: **Ted Demopoulos**
> Is VOIP Wiretapping a Privacy Threat?
> eWeek - Woburn,MA,USA
> . . . "This is another step in the erosion of personal privacy," said **Ted Demopoulos,** a leading IT consultant and professional speaker, based near Concord, NH, who . . .

These search engines do include results from blogs, but are not optimized to search blogs. The results of searches are returned in the order the search engine deems important, and a recent blog post or news item about your company may be buried on page eight of the results.

Google also has a blog-specific search that was released in beta in mid-September of 2005. We'll discuss Google's blog search later in this chapter. There are some rumors that other major general purpose search engines are working on blog-specific searches.

Search engines are continually changing and improving how they search and return results. There is an entire industry devoted to search engine optimization, or SEO, which attempts to get high rankings for specific Web pages and Web sites in the search engines. Techniques continue to evolve as search engine algorithms evolve. Getting a high ranking for popular search terms and products, which usually results in high visibility and traffic, is extremely difficult. Because search engines do not publicize their algorithms, SEO is seemingly partly magic. An in-depth discussion of SEO is beyond the scope of this book because changes occur too rapidly for print publication, but some useful basics will be introduced in Chapter 10.

It's important to distinguish between "natural" or "organic" search results, and paid placements. Paid placements can be bought, while organic results cannot. Paid placements are essentially a form of advertising. In the screen shot in Figure 4.1, the first result on top and the results on the right, labeled Sponsored Links, are paid placements. The other results are organic or natural results.

FIGURE 4.1 *Google Paid Placements*

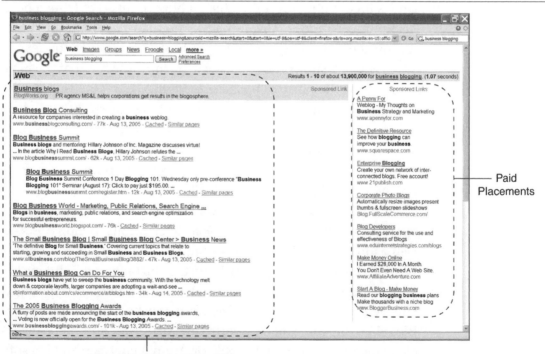

"Organic" or "Natural" Results

Paid Placements

Most general search engines have paid placements, including Google, Yahoo!, and MSN, as well as some specialized search engines, such as Technorati.

The two essential specialized search engines for checking on the blogosphere are Technorati and Daypop.

Technorati. Technorati describes itself as the authority on what's going on in the world of Web logs. It is a blog-specific search engine and currently tracks over 23.5 million blogs and 1.8 billion links between blogs; the numbers will undoubtedly be much higher when you read this. Technorati rates blogs by the number of links they have from other blogs, and has a top 100 list of the most popular blogs. Currently, Boing Boing: A Directory of Wonderful Things, is the most popular with almost 16,000 links. It only considers links from the home page of a blog, and this includes links from blogrolls. When a blog is linked to from a post, Technorati considers this link in its popularity rating only while it is on the home page; once it scrolls off it no longer counts.

Figure 4.2 shows the results of a Technorati search of the blogosphere for the phrase "business blogging."

A Technorati search of the blogosphere for sites that link to demop.com is shown in Figure 4.3. Notice the sponsored links, also known as paid placements or advertisements.

Technorati can search for specific words or phrases, sites that link to a specific URL, or specific Technorati Tags.

A Technorati Tag is a relatively recent innovation that allows applying simple category or subject descriptions to blog posts, as well as links and photos. For example, I could decide to tag my posts on business blogging with the tag "bizblogging," and my humorous posts as "humor" or "haha" or "funny" or anything I choose. Tags are not predefined but can be chosen on the fly. Blogging software that supports categories will automatically include tag information in the RSS or Atom feed. Users of blog software that doesn't support categories and RSS/Atom feeds can still

FIGURE 4.2 *A Technorati Search for "Business Blogging"*

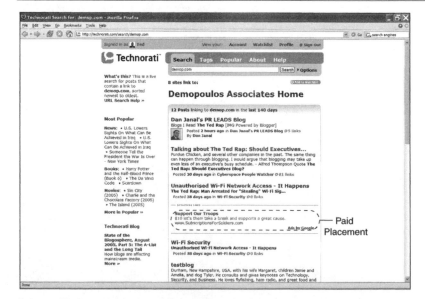

Search Results

Source: Technorati (www.technorati.com).

FIGURE 4.3 *Technorati Paid Placements*

Paid Placement

Source: Technorati (www.technorati.com).

use tags by adding a small piece of code that defines a link to the HTML of a blog post. The general format is:

```
<a href="http://technorati.com/tag/[tagname]" rel="tag">[tagname]</a>
```

For example the following code snippet added to a blog post tags it as "shave me," a tag name made up as an example.

```
<a href="http://technorati.com/tag/shave me" rel="tag">shave me</a>
```

The post will now display a link named "shave me" and clicking on it will display recent posts with the tag "shave me." Figure 4.4 shows a Technorati search of the blogosphere for the tag "security."

FIGURE 4.4 *Technorati Search on the Tag "Security"*

Source: Technorati (www.technorati.com).

Two additional features Technorati offers are a watchlist and a blog finder. Technorati Watchlist is a list of Technorati searches. As new matches for the search are found in the future, they are added to the watchlist. Watchlists can currently monitor URLs, which can represent a blog, as well as keywords. Watchlists can be accessed from a feedreader via an RSS feed or directly from Technorati.com.

In additional to Technorati search, Technorati also has a blog finder. Technorati Blog Finder returns entire blogs, instead of posts. Technorati Blog Finder is useful for finding blogs in areas in which you are interested, for example pharmacology, marketing, and technology. This can be useful for finding blogs that focus on your industry or interests. (See Figure 4.5.)

FIGURE 4.5 *Technorati Search for Blogs on Marketing*

Source: Technorati (www.technorati.com).

Daypop. Daypop is a current events search engine. It doesn't attempt to search the entire Internet, but concentrates on sites that update on a daily basis. Daypop refers to these as the "living Web" and it examines ("crawls") a human-edited list of approximately 59,000 news sites, blogs, and their associated RSS feeds on a daily basis. Major news sites like CNN and ABC are crawled every three hours.

Daypop allows you to search news, blogs, news and blogs, or just RSS feed headlines. Its advanced search engine allows you to search for information within a certain time range, specific languages, or even specific countries. Results can be displayed by relevance or date. An example of a search of "George W. Bush" sorted by date is shown in Figure 4.6.

Daypop tracks several items that can help determine trends. These include "Word Bursts," which are the increased use of certain words in blogs within the last couple of days and indicators of what is being blogged about heavily. Also tracked are "News Bursts," the increased use of certain words on front pages of news sites.

PubSub. PubSub is a fairly new free service that is short for publish and subscribe. Like everything on the Internet, it is still growing and evolving, but is already quite powerful and useful. It describes itself as a matching engine as opposed to a search engine. Typical search engines maintain a large database of what is on the Web, which they create by crawling the Web and indexing the information they find. They resolve queries against this database. PubSub does not store a database of Web information; instead it stores a database of persistent user queries and resolves them as it crawls the Web. A typical search engine returns historical information in a one-shot deal. PubSub returns future information as it's found on an ongoing basis.

PubSub crawls the Web examining information in RSS and Atom feeds. Although almost all blogs implement feeds, not all

FIGURE 4.6 *Daypop Search on "George W. Bush"*

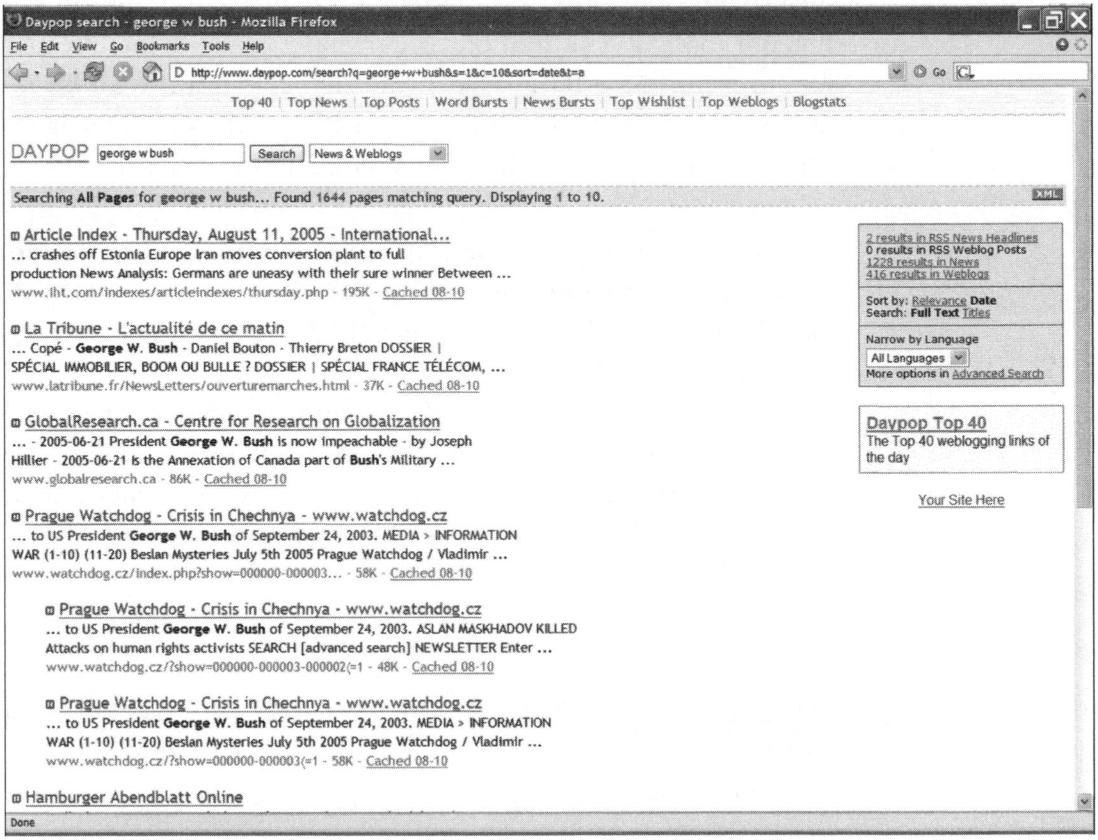

blogs have their entire posts in their feeds. Some have only post titles or partial text, which will limit what is found.

PubSub can limit searches to blogs, newsgroups, airport delays, press releases, and more. It can limit blog searches to the top 1 percent, 2 percent, 5 percent, 10 percent, 25 percent, or 75 percent of blogs as measured by LinkRanks. LinkRanks is PubSub's method of measuring the strength, persistence, and vitality of links, and are similar conceptually to the Technorati rank. LinkRanks only considers links in RSS and Atom feeds, which means links from blogrolls don't count. Also, links older than 30 days are not considered.

PubSub is very flexible in how it can return results. It can return results in real time via instant messaging if a user installs the PubSub toolbar. The tool bar is currently available for Internet Explorer and Mozilla Firefox browsers. The results can be returned to a feedreader via an Atom or RSS feed, as we'll see later. The user can also create browser shortcuts to view results.

BlogPulse. BlogPulse, a blog search engine and more, describes itself as an automated trend discovery system for blogs. It includes some fascinating tools such as Trend Search, Conversation Tracker, and BlogPulse Profiles. (See Figure 4.7.)

BlogPulse's Trend Search allows you to visually track "buzz" over time for certain key words, phrases, or links. For example, we see that approximately 3.5 percent of all blog posts mentioned Hurricane Katrina in early September, and approximately 0.5 percent by the end of September. (See Figure 4.8.)

FIGURE 4.7 *The BlogPulse Home Page*

Source: © Intelliseek, Inc. All Rights Reserved.

FIGURE 4.8 *BlogPulse Trend Search of "Hurricane Katrina"*

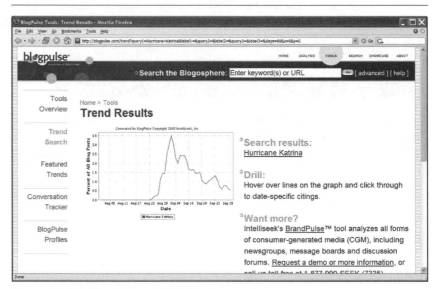

Source: © Intelliseek, Inc. All Rights Reserved.

BlogPulse Conversation Tracker allows tracking blogosphere conversations, which includes an original blog post, posts that have linked to it, posts that have linked to those posts, and so on.

BlogPulse Profiles allows you to get more information about a blog. Examining Seth Godin's blog in the screen shot in Figure 4.9, you can see its popularity increased in early September, that Seth posts an average of ten times a week, and his blog's BlogPulse rank. BlogPulse Profiles have much more information available as well. A BlogPulse rank is based on incoming links from other blogs' posts that are less than six months old. Links from blogrolls are not considered in a BlogPulse rank.

RSS search engines. RSS search engines search for information in RSS feeds. Some search Atom feeds as well. Examples of RSS search engines include Google Blog Search, Feedster, 2RSS.com, and Blogdigger.

FIGURE 4.9 *BlogPulse Profile for Seth's Blog*

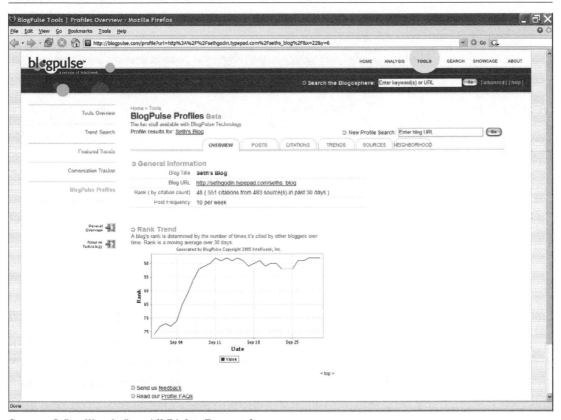

RSS search engines search only information in RSS feeds, and sometimes Atom feeds, just as PubSub does. Because most blogs implement feeds, these search engines can be very useful. It is important to realize, however, that not all blogs have their entire posts in their RSS feeds. Some may have only post titles or partial text, which will limit what is found.

The screen shot in Figure 4.10 shows a search of Dearborn Trade Publishing using Feedster. Note that the results are shown by date, but can also be shown by relevance, as defined by Feedster.

FIGURE 4.10 *Feedster Search on "Dearborn Trade Publishing"*

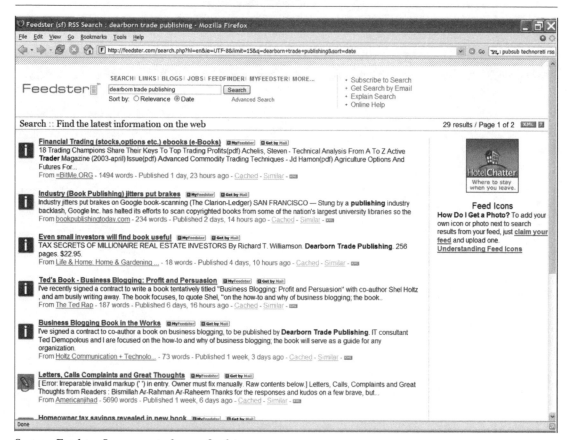

Source: Feedster Incorporated www.feedster.com.

Feedster, perhaps not surprisingly, also allows you to subscribe to searches so you are notified of new matches as they are found. The new matches can be sent via e-mail or RSS. This is similar to PubSub's functionality and Technorati Watchlists.

The screen shot in Figure 4.11 shows a search of Dearborn Trade Publishing using Google Blog Search. Note that the results are shown by relevance, which is the default for Google Blog Search. Although Google is a newcomer to the blog search field, its skill in determining relevance among search results is an enormous advantage.

FIGURE 4.11 *Google Blog Search (Beta) on "Dearborn Trade Publishing"*

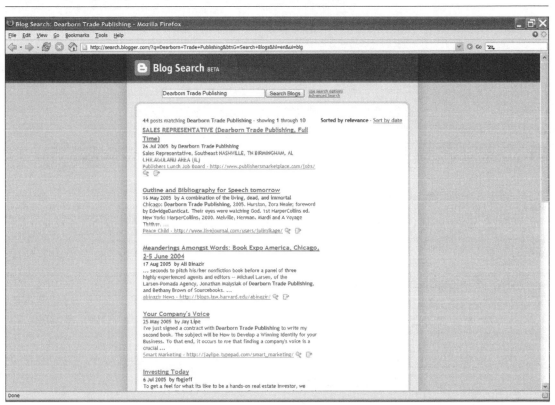

Google Blog Search also allows you to subscribe to searches so you are notified of new matches as they are found. The new matches can be accessed via RSS or Atom.

MONITORING SPECIFIC BLOGS

Search engines are great for searching for specific words and phrases, including names of companies and people. However, sometimes we don't want to search. We want to read specific periodicals, newspapers, and books. Important blogs are now also on the "must read" list. For example, just as many investors read the *Wall Street Journal,* many software professionals read Scobleizer, Joel on Software, and Slashdot. Many political pundits read Instapundit, Daily Kos, and Talking Points Memo, and many gadget lovers and those in the gadget industry read Engadget and Gizmodo.

There are a couple of major differences between traditional print media and blogs that affect your ability to monitor them: there are a lot more blogs, and they don't publish on a regular schedule. Important bloggers may post several times a day, or only when they have something important to say. Both these differences make blogs potentially more difficult to keep up with. As many have said before, "So much information, so little time." Information overload is a serious problem for most of us.

Many of us, including Shel and Ted, follow dozens of Web sites, including news sites and blogs. Going to each site with a browser to see if there is anything new of interest is extremely time-consuming. Some of these sites have periodic e-mails or newsletters that can be subscribed to for updates, but many of us really don't want any more e-mail. Most Internet users get more than enough e-mail.

What if there was some type of utility that would allow us to conveniently and quickly see what's new on *all* of the sites we're interested in, and let us click through to any particular item we want to examine in detail?

Of course there are such utilities, and they are called feedreaders, newsreaders, or sometimes news aggregators.

They "read" RSS feeds you have expressed interest in by subscribing, and show you what's new in those feeds. Because subscribing to an RSS feed merely means that your feedreader is reading an RSS feed for that site, there is no chance that subscribing will result in any kind of spam.

There are many popular feedreaders, including SharpReader, FeedDemon, and Feedreader, which are stand-alone applications, and Bloglines, Pluck, and My Yahoo!, which are Web-based.

Figure 4.12 is a screen shot of the popular Bloglines feedreader. On the left side, we see the feeds that are subscribed to. Feeds listed include A New Marketing Commentator, a shel of my former self, Amazon.com–Books: Professional & Technical, and many more. Feeds that are shown in bold have unviewed items. The number of items, typically posts, is shown in parentheses next to the feed name. We can display the items in any feed by clicking on it. Displayed in the main screen is Neville Hobson's blog Nevon. Note that the number of subscribers via Bloglines, 97, is shown in the top middle of the main screen.

Clicking on the feed Schneier on Security displays Bruce Schneier's blog as shown in Figure 4.13.

We can go to the blog itself or any specific posts by clicking on the links in the blog's displayed text. Figure 4.14 shows the results of clicking on the post title *Giving the U.S. Military the Power to Conduct Domestic Surveillance.*

FIGURE 4.12 *The Bloglines Feedreader Displaying the NevOn Blog*

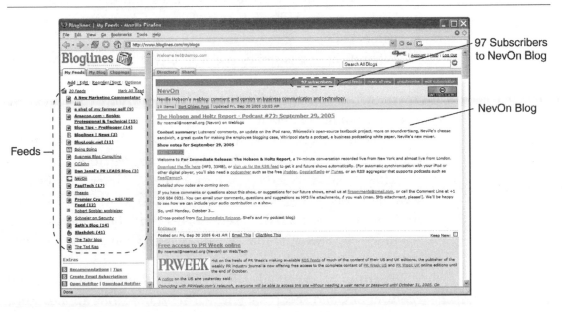

FIGURE 4.13 *The Bloglines Feedreader Displaying the Schneier on Security Blog*

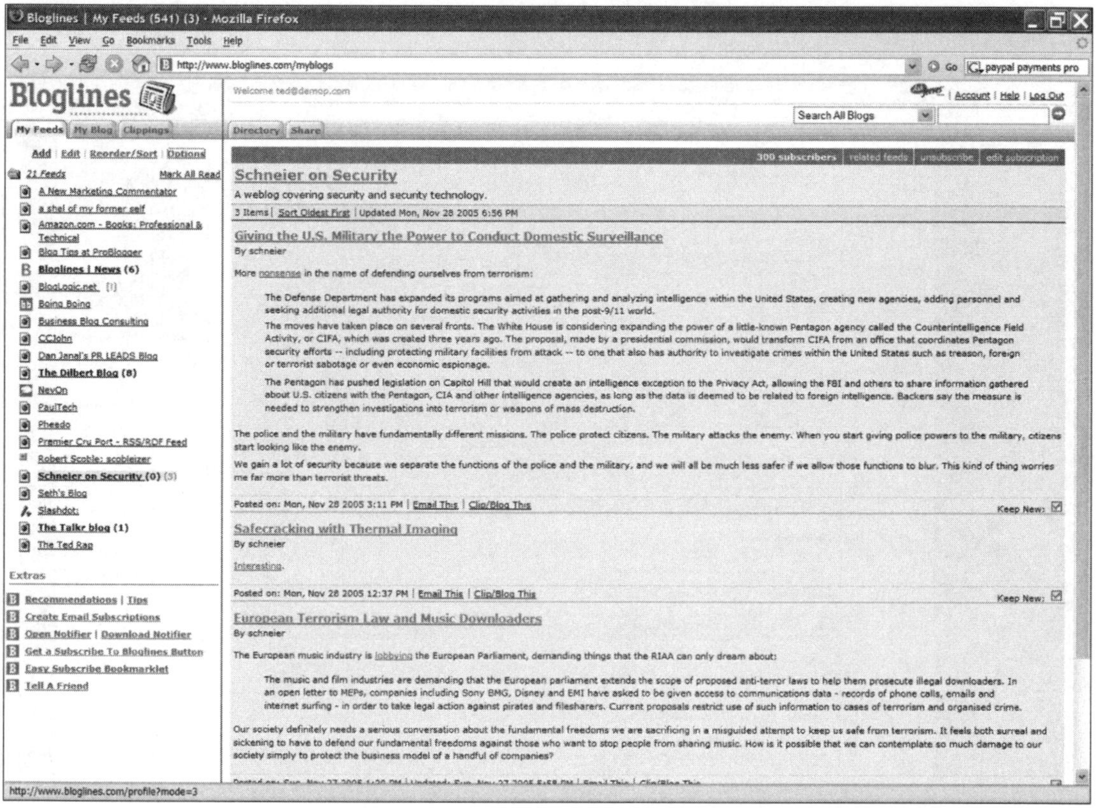

Among other things, this allows us to see any comments and trackbacks to that post.

Bloglines also includes general-purpose and blog-specific search engine capabilities, which search blogs that are subscribed to by at least one Bloglines user.

SUMMARY

The importance of blogs is rapidly increasing in business, and has reached the point that intelligent organizations need to be

FIGURE 4.14 *Bruce Schneier's Schneier on Security Blog*

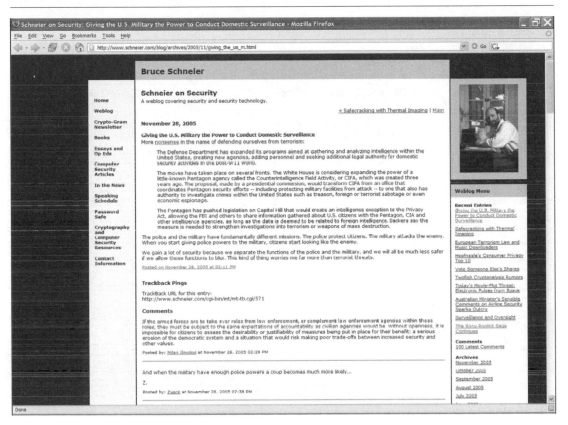

monitoring what is being said in the blogosphere. Your competitors probably are and so should you!

Once you are monitoring important conversations in the blogosphere, you might want to consider joining it. You can certainly join in a limited fashion by making comments on other's blogs, and you can take the full plunge into what blogs can offer your organization by starting one or more blogs of your own. In the next chapter, we discuss tapping into the blogosphere.

TAPPING INTO
THE BLOGOSPHERE

Ultimately, as valuable as blogging can be for your company, you don't need a blog in order to take advantage of the blogosphere. In the last chapter, we talked about monitoring the blogosphere. Based on the results of these efforts, you can engage in a number of practices that will help you get your messages out and influence bloggers, their readers, and the non-readers who are influenced by them.

By becoming an active participant in the blogosphere—beyond your own blog—you engage in conversation with potential customers as well as those who influence potential customers: the bloggers they read. The blogosphere is rich with examples of independent blogs that serve a company's goals when the organization works with the blogger in support of the blogger's efforts. Essentially, the company's goals and those of the blogger can be jointly served when the two work collaboratively, which, of course, is consistent with the philosophical underpinnings of blogging. Bloggers with whom you have a solid relationship can become an extension of your communication efforts that is frequently more credible than anything you could communicate in a press release.

PITCHING BLOGGERS

We have spoken at some length about the role of blogs and bloggers in the context of the traditional media. Just as newspaper and magazine writers influence readers, bloggers also wield influence over the readers of their material. Knowing this, you can figure out which bloggers influence *your* target audience and work to establish a special relationship with these bloggers so their blogs serve as a conduit for your messages.

This section is titled "Pitching Bloggers" because most organizations understand the notion of pitching the media. In fact, bloggers would most likely bristle at the notion of being pitched. They could react by turning against you if they feel they are being used by the organization. That's why the approach to take is really more one of establishing a relationship, a partnership.

Consider a blog such as Treonauts. This is a blog written as a full-time activity by a blogger dedicated to the Treo cell phone. Treonauts has become a primary source of information about the Treo, devoured regularly by Treo owners and wannabe Treo owners. PalmOne, which makes the Treo, has established a connection with the blog, feeding information and making its representatives available for questions. PalmOne no doubt is frequently unhappy with content this independent "bloguide" publishes, but it would be to the company's detriment to curtail its relationship and have no access to Treonaut's audience. Better to get some content out to a dedicated audience and put up with some material you'd rather didn't appear than not have a relationship with the blogger at all!

General Motors was able to take advantage of an existing blogger when it responded to a firestorm of controversy that erupted when the company withdrew advertising from the *Los Angeles Times* following some unfavorable and (according to GM) biased and inaccurate reporting on its company. Rather than address the *Times'* alleged inaccuracies in its own blog, the company provided information to a popular and influential auto-focused blog, Automoblog, which lent credibility to the response. GM communications executive Gary Grates also addressed the rationale for withdrawing the advertising from the *Times* on the GM FastLane blog. While the post drew a detailed and vehement comment opposing the move, many subsequent comments responded by supporting GM's decision.

Here's one more example of pitching bloggers that has met with phenomenal success: book reviews. In the world of publishing, there are precious few column-inches in the traditional media dedicated to reviews of books. Book critics are inclined to read and review books by well-known authors, or those with the biggest advertising and marketing budgets. Smaller books with limited audiences hardly ever get attention in the *New York Times Review of Books,* or even the book review sections in smaller newspapers' Sunday supplements. Book publicists have turned to blogs in a big way, identifying bloggers whose efforts are focused on the same audiences at whom the books they are promoting are targeted. Shel, for example, has received several books on public relations, podcasting, marketing, and blogging for review on his blog and through his PR-focused podcast. Bloggers are delighted to get free books—particularly when those books are related directly to their interests—and are often happy to share their thoughts about the books with their readers (as long as they are not expected to report favorably on books they didn't like!).

Some guidelines for pitching bloggers include the following:

- Carefully and thoroughly read the blog you plan to pitch to. You should have a clear and complete understanding of the blog's theme and the bloggers' interests, issues, peeves, and approaches to addressing each.

- When you contact the blogger, make sure you approach it as a conversation, not as a pitch. Address the blogger by his or her name. Rather than tell him that he *must* read your book or review your product, tell him *why* the book or product would be of interest to him.

- While your pitch should be personal, don't be overfamiliar. While you probably learned a lot about the blogger from reading the blog, the blogger knows nothing about you. A blogger could easily resent this faux intimacy.

- Be candid about what you want from the blogger. Make sure you disclose your relationship with your organization at the outset.

- Keep your pitch short. If you're pitching a blogger, odds are others are, too. Some bloggers get five, ten, even 50 pitches every day. If yours is brief and to the point, it's more likely the blogger will give it a look.

- Start by referring to a post from the blogger. It's important for the blogger to know you've read the blog's material. You can even initiate a conversation by posting a comment in response to one of the blogger's posts.

- Never ask a blogger to link to your company's site or any company content, such as a press release or a product page. No blogger wants to be perceived as a shill for a company. However, providing links as part of your pitch *is* important. Bloggers *love* links.

- Don't mass-pitch bloggers. You may send the same press release to a list of mainstream media correspondents, but each contact with a blogger should be unique, tailored to the interests and approaches of the blog.

- Make the contact personal, such as an e-mail to the blogger or even a phone call if you can find the phone number. Don't post a request to the blog.

- Don't follow up with the blogger. (Reporters for mainstream media publications hate this, too, by the way.) If you want to find out if the blogger has written about you, read the blog. If the blogger is interested in pursuing the relationship, he or she will let you know. Posting a subsequent request in a month, however, won't be seen as being too pushy.
- Be prepared for bloggers to post your pitch. As strong believers in transparency, bloggers are well known for publishing the pitches they receive in the interest of ensuring that readers know what's behind their posts.
- Present your pitch as a story. Bloggers prefer to tell stories rather than simply duplicate a product announcement.
- Include contact information. It may seem like the most basic of all rules, but it's surprising how many pitches to bloggers don't include at least one of the following elements: location, phone number, e-mail address, blog URL (if you have one), company URL. You can also provide links to FAQs, team biographies, and other resources that the blogger you're pitching may find useful.
- Don't expect bloggers to abide by journalists' rules—or even understand the lingo. For example, asking a blogger to honor an embargo is likely to result in the immediate publication of the news. Even if you use layman's terms to make your request, "Could you please not post anything about this until Tuesday?" isn't likely to set well with the blogger.

PAY-FOR-PUBLICITY PROGRAMS

Quite a lot of attention was focused on a program launched by a content management software company called Marqui that took advantage of the blogosphere in a unique and, some would say, unethical way. Because it generated so much controversy, it's worth looking at, even if we don't advise that you adopt its principles.

Marqui solicited bloggers who would write about its product in exchange for a fee. The company called its program a trust-based blogging program. The program's approach was outlined in a company press release: "The premise of Marqui's PayBloggers program is simple. Participating bloggers are required to write about Marqui on a regular basis and display a logo indicating that they are paid by the company. In order to preserve bloggers' integrity, Marqui pays each blogger for the duration of the contract, regardless of the positive or negative nature of the feedback. All Marqui-sponsored posts, a list of participating bloggers, and full terms and conditions of the program are available on Marqui's Web site at http://www.marqui.com/Paybloggers/."

From Marqui's standpoint, the program was a rousing success. According to president and CEO Stephen King, "Not only did we benefit from a massive amount of attention and valuable product feedback immediately after the launch, we've also been able to maintain a consistent level of awareness among influential bloggers and journalists. Furthermore, we've been instrumental in changing the way many marketers view the Web, which is extremely appropriate given the nature of our product."

Many in the blogosphere, however, were highly critical of the program. Stowe Boyd, a columnist for the Corante network of blogs, wrote, "While blog advertising has become standard practice, it starts to get cheesy when the blogger is not necessarily writing entries based on his passions, interests, and insights. He's being influenced to put things into his blog because he's being paid to do it. That violates a basic operating principle of the blogosphere."

Boyd—an influential blogger in his own right—has a valid point, but it's not the only one. While the Marquis' bloggers may have disclosed their relationship, the act of writing about Marqui was hardly objective, because none of these bloggers gave the same kind of attention to Marquis' competitors. While this, no doubt, was fine from Marquis' standpoint, it didn't necessarily help the reputation of the bloggers who took the company's money.

Marqui is quick to disagree with the objections raised to its program, saying that there is no evidence to suggest any of the bloggers' reputations were tarnished by the program. The company also points out that it's hard to question the objectivity of the bloggers considering that not all of the posts could be considered favorable. One blogger sharply criticized a Marqui white paper, and another frequently commented on the ambiguous messaging on the company's Web site.

Not surprisingly, Marqui also strongly disagrees with Boyd and others who question the ethics of the program. From Marqui's perspective, the program's benefits—and one of the advantages of tapping into the blogosphere in general—is that it gives the public an opportunity to have an interactive discussion and reach its own conclusions. This is in sharp contrast to more traditional marketing or advertising tactics, which don't necessarily encourage or facilitate a two-way conversation.

While the Marqui approach is certainly available to you, approach it with extreme caution and only if you can stand the heat from the many bloggers who will attack your actions.

GENERATING SOME BUZZ

If you get to know the blogosphere and have something to contribute—even if it is not your own content—you can still generate some buzz without getting blogging purists up in arms over your actions. Nobody minds if you reap some benefits by doing something bloggers like.

The producers of the movie *Serenity* understood this when they spread tickets to movie previews among bloggers on the condition that they review the film. Nobody was required to write a *good* review; the only condition was to write some kind of review. Of course, most of those who clamored for the tickets were fans of the film's director and the cancelled television series on which

it was based, and they blogged prodigiously about it. The producers could rest fairly well assured that most of the reviews would be glowing and that they would influence readers to go see it. Bloggers got free tickets to a movie they wanted to see with no compromise of their ethics; the movie producers generated tons of positive buzz on the blogosphere.

There are plenty of opportunities like this that require you to understand the bloggers in your market sector and figure out a mutually beneficial offer. For example, book authors have turned to the blogosphere to enhance the limited marketing provided by publishers. Shel has been sent several books of interest to him in exchange for a review, positive or negative. The books match Shel's interest because the authors want to reach *his* audience. In one case, he produced a podcast review of a book on podcasting! The author of the podcasting book got a good review while Shel got a book he wanted to read. (In case you're wondering, yes, Ted and Shel will most definitely employ this approach in the marketing of *this* book. In fact, we wouldn't be the least bit surprised to find out that *you* bought this book because you read about it on a blog.)

ADVERTISING

A common fantasy expressed by many bloggers is the dream of blogging full-time. Most of those that have been able to turn this reality into a fantasy are the ones who have accepted advertising on their blogs.

Ads on a blog are pretty much the same as ads on a Web site. A graphic appears in a prominent (or, at least, a visible) spot on the home page and when clicked directs the visitor to the advertiser's Web site.

Unlike the Marquis program explained above, most bloggers wouldn't have too much of a problem with paid advertising as long as acceptance of the ad doesn't influence the blogger's content. Most bloggers won't tolerate an advertiser trying to control their content.

Advertising rates for blogs are not calculated by any kind of science at this point. The more readers a blogger has, the more you'll pay. One of the top blogs, Daily Kos, charges only $800 per week for ads. On the other hand, a podcast aimed at endurance athletes has earned up to $4,000 per month for ads that reach a highly targeted and extremely influential audience. Companies such as Gatorade and Fleet Sports have ponied up the funds to reach that market.

One way to tap into advertising without having to track down pertinent bloggers is through Google's AdWords program. In the Google program, you pay for a link to your site to appear on a page bearing the results of a related search. Because your link is relevant to the searcher's interests, it is more likely to be clicked on. In addition to appearing in Google's own search results, the company enters into affinity arrangements with bloggers and Web site owners. In exchange for letting AdWords appear on their sites, Google rewards the bloggers with a fee for each AdWords link clicked. The AdWords that appear in a blog are related to the content of the blog, ensuring greater interest from readers. AdWords has been a huge success for Google and could make sense as a way to get some visibility in the blogosphere.

One issue to keep in mind with AdWords, though, is that the blogger has no control over the ads that appear. Given the content of any one post, AdWords could generate an ad the blogger might consider unsavory or inappropriate, and there's nothing the blogger could do about it.

SUMMARY

A range of opportunities is available to you in the blogosphere, even if you don't have a blog. But those opportunities expand exponentially if you *do* have a blog. Approaches and techniques for making money from blogs is the theme of our next chapter.

C h a p t e r

6

HOW TO MAKE MONEY
WITH BLOGS

Although some blogs may be started and exist primarily for the purpose of generating revenue, most business blogs have a role in supporting a pre-existing venture. It is important to remember the prime role of a blog in an organization. Generating revenue in a matter inconsistent with an organization's primary mission can weaken an organization's reputation and brand. As a blatant example, a nonprofit organization devoted to improving health care would not want to have advertisements for tobacco-based products, whether inadvertent or not. Most Fortune 500 companies would not want to advertise sexual aids, regardless of the profit potential. A major name brand PC manufacturer would not want endorse discount brands.

However, there often are potential ways a business blog can earn money in line with its primary mission. For example, an organization can endorse, and perhaps earn money from the sales of, complementary products from which it believes its customers would benefit. A product-based organization can advertise recommended services it endorses in its product space, perhaps consulting or training on its products from trusted third parties.

There are several potential ways to make money with blogs. We consider both explicit and implicit methods. An example of an explicit method is running advertisements on a blog or asking for donations. An explicit method is usually obvious to all that see it: something is being done specifically for remuneration. Implicit methods are subtler. Examples include highlighting your products or services and building your credibility though insightful postings. There is not always a clear-cut difference between all implicit or explicit methods. Would devoting some screen space in the sidebar or perhaps dedicating a few posts to featuring or explaining a partner's complementary service or product, its value, and how many of your customers could benefit from it be explicit or implicit? Would the reader know or even care if there were commissions or other remuneration involved?

Let's be absolutely clear. There are some blogs with a large amount of traffic—millions of visitors and page views per month—and some of these blogs are effectively monetizing their traffic. Darren Rowse, who writes the Problogger.net blog among others, reports making over $100,000 in advertising revenue alone during a recent 12-month period. While perhaps an insignificant sum for a Fortune 500 company, it is significant for an individual and many small businesses. We must also be clear that there are probably very few blogs making that kind of actual cash now. However, there may be many blogs that are creating that kind of value in increased customer retention, sales, loyalty, etc.

In some blogs, explicit methods of generating income would seem extremely out of place. Could you imagine a Fortune 500 CEO blog running Google AdSense advertisements or perhaps advertisements for unrelated products? They would be out of place and not in tune with most Fortune 500 corporate cultures and sensibilities. Then again, blogs are a new medium and what may seem absurd today may be commonplace tomorrow. After all, even the thought of using the Internet for any commercial purposes was seen as immoral and almost perverted not long ago. Certainly the idea of advertising a complementary product, whether via a paid advertisement or not, seems quite reasonable for almost any organization. For example, a General Motors blog having a graphic in the sidebar of the motor oil it recommends, or a Microsoft blog highlighting a Microsoft training partner in a post is quite reasonable.

Implicit methods of making money via a blog are more likely to be universally accepted. Robert Scoble writing about great new features in upcoming Microsoft products in his Scobleizer blog and General Motors' Smallblock Engine Blog discussing the results of J. D. Power and Associates 2005 Vehicle Dependability Study and how General Motors vehicles fared are examples of implicit methods.

ADVERTISEMENTS

Advertising is the promotion of products, services, and ideas. Most advertising is paid and has a clearly identified sponsor. Many blogs carry advertisements, ranging from the ubiquitous Google AdSense that almost any blog or Web site can carry, to targeted corporate advertising on select high-traffic sites. Organizations can even carry their own formal advertisements on their blogs. Admittedly, blog advertising is very much in its infancy, although the *Wall Street Journal,* Paramount Pictures, the *New Yorker,* and many others have used it.

Effective advertising is all about trial and error. Advertisements that work in one market or for one product may not be as effective elsewhere. Often an effective advertisement will lose or gain effectiveness over time. Sometimes small changes in an advertisement will result in surprising changes in effectiveness.

We'll look at a few types of advertising that can appear on blogs first, and then consider the placing of advertisements in RSS and Atom feeds.

Advertiser Payment Plans

There are several schemes for charging for advertising, from a straightforward fixed price for running an advertisement for a given amount of time, to various pay-for-performance options.

Pay per impression. With pay per impression, you are paid for the number of times the advertisement is displayed. More traffic automatically means more payments. The amount paid is often described in terms of cost per thousand impressions, or CPM. This somewhat confusing acronym uses the Roman numeral "M" for thousand. Banner advertisements often are based on a pay-per-impression scheme.

Pay per click. With pay per click, payment is only incurred when visitors click the advertisements on your site. Advertisements must be carefully chosen to match the visitors to the site or a very low click rate will occur. In advertising terminology, there is a low conversion rate—the percentage of visitors who make you money—if the advertisements are not carefully targeted. Google AdSense is an example of pay per click.

Pay per sale. As in pay per click, visitors must click the advertisement but they also need to make a purchase. Like the pay-per-click method, advertisements must be carefully chosen to suit the target audience of your site. The Amazon.com Associates program is an example of pay per sale.

Pay per placement. Pay per placement is a payment scheme similar to print media and billboards. The advertiser pays for the privilege of having the advertisement placed in a particular location. The payment is the same regardless of how many people view it, click on it, or are motivated to buy. Blogsads.com advertisements, which we'll look at later, operate on pay per placement.

Reasons Not to Have Advertisements on a Blog

There are at least two significant reasons a blog might not want to have advertisements. The first reason is that some people feel that advertisements cheapen a blog, especially a business blog. Could you imagine Google AdSense advertisements on a Fortune 500 company's Web site or blog? Ted didn't initially run advertisements because he is promoting business/technical consulting services and keynote speeches and felt that having somewhat arbitrary advertisements that paid on average a few coins per click would appear unprofessional. Ted did eventually implement Google AdSense and Amazon.com Associates advertisements on his blog as well as others, primarily because he was interested in experimenting with advertising on blogs. The feedback was only positive. Some people commented that the advertisements made the blog seem more professional, more like a trusted newspaper or periodical. No one felt the advertisements detracted from the blog, which surprised him. He would never consider running advertisements on his company's Web site, but on blogs they do not seem out of place. Perhaps this shouldn't be surprising as blogs, even business blogs, are a less formal medium than business Web sites.

The second reason not to have advertisements on a blog is because they take up valuable real estate. The space occupied by an advertisement can often be used far more effectively in other ways. For example, an organization could use space otherwise occupied by ads for highlighting one of its products or services, which is really a form of advertisement itself, or perhaps something that helps in branding the organization. For example, what would help Demopoulos Associates more, advertisement for somewhat arbitrary third party products on Ted's blog, or perhaps a photo of this book? Unless the ads were making significant revenue, certainly of the order of several thousand dollars a month, that space has far more valuable uses. Demopoulos Associates is a very small shop; the space would be far more valuable in terms of dollars for an organization of any significant size. Other items that would be probably more useful in Ted's case would include a link to his latest security survey and a link to streaming audio of one of his recent keynote speeches. Screen real estate is valuable! It can even be valuable to leave some of it blank to help focus attention on the "important stuff."

Google AdSense

Google AdSense is one of the most popular advertising programs on the Internet and perhaps in the world. Google AdSense can place context-sensitive advertisements on any blog or Web page. There is very little control over what advertisements are displayed, although you can control where on the screen they appear. You can exclude specific advertisements by URL, so you can exclude competitors' advertisements if you like, as well as any advertisements you might find objectionable. Google determines which advertisements to place on your page by context—by looking at what else is on that page. Your AdSense account has money credited every time someone clicks on an advertisement, anywhere from a few pennies to a few dollars (i.e., pay per click). Google AdWords is the other side of Google's advertisement equation. With AdWords, people pay to have traffic delivered to them via clicks on AdSense advertisements.

An interesting variation on Google advertisements is the use of "link units." Each link unit displays a list of topics based on the content of your site. When users click on one of these topics, they see a page of related Google advertisements. Payment is received not for clicking on the topics, but for clicking on the advertisements on the resulting page.

What we have been discussing so far is the popular AdSense for Content. There is also Google AdSense for Search, which displays a small Google search box and pays revenue when any of the sponsored results are clicked. Google also has a Top Queries reporting feature that lets you see the top 25 searches performed on your site. Options for the Google search box include a toggle switch that allows searching the entire Internet or just your site.

Google takes its AdSense terms of service extremely seriously—too seriously, some believe. Any violation, even as simple as clicking on one of your ads to see if it works, or saying "visit our sponsors," can result in immediate banishment from the AdSense program. Often the grounds for dismissal are alleged "invalid" clicks with no further explanation. There is no appeal, there are no borderline cases, there are no minor infractions, and often there is little description of why the banishment occurred. Google is judge, jury, and executioner. And they take any accrued money out of your AdSense account too!

Small changes to Google advertisements can make a very big difference in results. Although placing the advertisements in different places in Ted's blog didn't make much of a difference, merely removing the default border from the advertisements more than quadrupled the number of "clicks," and hence the revenue. Changing the text color to more closely match that of his blog also had a very significant effect on the number of clicks. Google's A look inside Google AdSense blog, http://www.adsense.blogspot.com/, offers advice, as well as AdSense optimization tips for members of the AdSense program.

Others

Amazon.com Associates advertisements are also fairly popular on blogs. Amazon.com advertisements do not have the context-sensitive feature of Google AdSense, but they allow far more control in what is advertised. Specific books and other products can be advertised and products can be automatically chosen based on product categories or keywords. Amazon.com Associates advertisements are based on pay per sale (i.e., money is only earned when a reader completes a purchase). Both Shel and Ted use Amazon.com to advertise professional books they endorse.

Blogads is a company specializing in blog advertising. It connects bloggers with advertisers. Advertisements cost up to $5,000 per placement per week although most are much less. Blogads describes blog readers as hyper-literate, highly networked, influential and affluent, and warns that advertisements that work well on nonblog sites may underperform on blogs; they are a different medium that needs different approaches. Advertisements can combine a small image and up to 300 characters of text, with multiple links. Bloggers need an invitation to join, and Blogads states that the average blogger earns $50 per month, and some earn more than $5,000 per month.

CrispAds is another company that connects bloggers and advertisers. Its graphical advertisements range from over $16,000 per placement per month to a few dollars a month. All bloggers are invited to join CrispAds and are listed in its catalog to attract graphical advertisements sponsors. While waiting for potential graphical advertisers, keyword-targeted pay-per-click text advertisements are displayed. CrispAds pays bloggers via PayPal on a monthly basis when balances are over $5. Large payments are sent by check. Currently, anyone can join the CrispAds program, and bloggers set their price for graphical advertisements. CrispAds automatically are added to any RSS and Atom feeds.

AFFILIATE PROGRAMS

We'll define an affiliate program as a practice of paying a finder's fee for introducing new business. With this definition, many programs could be called either affiliate or advertising programs, or both. Affiliate programs certainly have a lot in common and a lot of overlap with advertising. We could call Amazon.com Associates a pay-per-sale affiliate program, and Google AdSense a pay-per-click affiliate program if we'd like. From our perspective the semantics don't matter; we're just looking at various techniques of making money from blogs.

Pay per sale is the most common affiliate program, although other payment schemes such pay per click and pay per lead are also common. Pay per lead pays a fee for each new sales lead generated, whether or not it results in an actual sale. Pay for performance is another term sometimes used, and eclipses pay per sale, click, and lead.

Many affiliate programs are single tier: you make money for each sale, click, or lead you generate. A double-tier program is one where you are also paid for any additional affiliates you get to join the program. You may get a set fee, a percentage of their revenue, or both. Multitier programs also exist, where you also get some revenue from anyone who joins the affiliate program via someone you got to join the affiliate program. Unfortunately, some multitier (and double-tier) affiliate programs concentrate on getting more people into the program rather than actual sales, and some of these are simply Ponzi schemes.

There are thousands of affiliate programs. Well-known and sizable ones include LinkShare and Commission Junction, which represent multiple merchants. Also, many electronic shopping cart programs, used for selling items from Web sites and discussed later, support producing affiliate links, which are essentially mini-affiliate programs.

Corporate Advertising

A blog with an established track record can directly pursue corporations and other organizations and attempt to sell them advertising or revenue. This is similar to selling advertising through Blogads, CrispAds, and others, but cuts out the middleman.

A company's blog could have advertisements for its own products as well. For example, GM's FastLane blog could have advertisements for the Solstace, and Sun Microsystems' Jonathan's Blog could have advertisements for its Sun Fire E25K server hardware. It is doubtful that anyone would find this inappropriate.

DONATIONS

Blogs can ask for donations. Why would someone donate to a blog and when would it be appropriate?

There are at least two significant reasons one would donate to a blog. One reason is because the reader likes the blog and wants to help support it. A blog that accepts donations could be one of many types or genres of blogs, but it would be most appropriate for a noncommercial or very small business blog that provides useful information or entertainment. It is hard to imagine a blog associated with a successful business asking for donations, except perhaps for a good cause.

Blogs of many nonprofit and philanthropic organizations can legitimately and reasonably ask for donations. Many of these organizations depend in large part or even entirely on donations, so asking for donations from one of their blogs would be entirely appropriate. Donations could even be requested for specific targeted causes, such as "to help support this blog and get the word out" or to fund specific charitable causes, whether long term, such as feeding and clothing the needy, or shorter term, such as to help survivors of specific disasters.

PayPal makes it easy to accept donations; donations are a feature included in Web site payments standards, and it even provides a "donations" button. Amazon.com also supports donations for blogs and other Web sites via the Amazon Honor System™. Of course, any blog that supports online commerce, or is affiliated with a Web site that does, can directly implement an online donation system.

SYNDICATION FEEDS

An increasing number of blog readers are reading blogs via RSS and Atom feeds. This includes people using feedreaders as well as feed-aware browsers such as Firefox and Opera. Certainly Microsoft's support of RSS and Atom in Internet Explorer 7.0 and Windows Vista are significant factors driving the acceptance of RSS and Atom feeds by ordinary Internet users.

Some blogs derive significant revenue from advertising and affiliate programs; however, readers accessing content via RSS or Atom do not see traditional Web-based advertisements and affiliate links unless they click through to the originating blog. It is not surprising that advertisements and affiliate links are starting to appear in feeds with more frequency.

Also, feed advertising can be an alternative to or supplement e-mail–based advertising. Feed advertising is entirely opt-in and has a 100 percent delivery rate. In contrast, e-mail–based advertising has multiple problems, including spam filters and e-mail overload. Many requested e-mails are never delivered due to over-aggressive spam filters and many delivered e-mails are never opened due to information overload. Advertising in feeds is in its infancy, but it is clear that feeds are a much different medium than Web sites and blogs, and different techniques will be needed for success with advertising.

There are several methods to get advertisements and affiliate links, and even requests for donations, into feeds. RSS and Atom feed files can be manually edited. Some advertising programs such as CrispAds automatically add their advertisements to feeds. Feedburner .com is a service that can add advertisements and affiliate links to your feed. Some blogging software, for example Blogger, will allow you to directly add advertisements and affiliate links to feeds.

SELL YOUR SERVICES AND PRODUCTS

Presumably, people reading a blog have some interest or connection with the author or authors, or at least some significant common ground and interests. If it is a business blog, some of the readers are probably already customers, and many of the rest are potential customers. This constitutes a prequalified group to sell to if there ever was one. One could ask, "Why bombard them with Google AdSense ads, affiliate links, and advertisements for others, when you could be highlighting your own organization and its services or products?"

Blogs can have information in the sidebar and perhaps the header and footer area highlighting the organization and its various products and services. This information can include explicit advertisements for the organization and offers to sell products and services as well as other subtler implicit methods of promoting the organization. These can include links to various places in the organization's main Web site that readers may be interested in, such as product plans and specifications, user case studies, upcoming events, surveys, etc. The blogroll can include other blogs from the organizations as well as blogs of "fans" of the organization. There can be pictures or simple graphics of products or planned products, links to product reviews and discussions, streaming or other audio as well as video files, and other supporting material. Use your imagination! This is not a one-size-fits-all scenario; different organizations will have different wants and needs, as well as different cultures and norms and a sense of what is appropriate. What make sense for a solo entrepreneur named "Crazy Teddy" may differ enormously from a large conservative charity.

Posts can also highlight an organization and its offerings, as long as the opinions and information are authentic. If all the posts that reference the company sound like a nonstop pep rally or marketing-speak, the blog will simply not gain widespread trust and be effective. Of course, there is nothing wrong with focusing on the positive, as long as controversies are squarely and honestly dealt with as well. Consider Robert Scoble's Scobleizer blog, for example. He tells his readers very straightforwardly what he loves about Microsoft, as well as what he doesn't. If there are products, initiatives, etc., he dislikes or is unsure about, he makes that clear. This helps his credibility enormously. He is widely accepted as honest and credible, and also extremely widely read.

SELL OTHER COMPANIES' SERVICES AND PRODUCTS

Just as a blog can highlight as well as sell an organization's own products and services, it can do the same for other organizations' products and services. Highlighting complementary products, services, and other organizations can be very effective and can add value to the reader. Honest assessments of add-on products, complementary services, and partner services can be very useful to customers and potential customers as well.

ACCEPTING PAYMENTS ON A BLOG

In order to actually sell products from a blog or Web site, it is necessary to have some mechanism for users to indicate what they want to buy, and to be able to accept payment in some form, most commonly credit cards. Many of these mechanisms require more functionality than most blogging solutions provide. Because most business blogs are associated with an organization's Web site, this is not typically an issue. A Web site is often required to store product pages and descriptions, custom code, customer lists, etc. It is possible to do some simple sales directly from a blog without an associated Web site. For example, a blog's sidebar could contain a description and picture of a product as well a "buy" button, perhaps using PayPal described below. There are also turnkey stores available, such as those offered by Yahoo!, that combine Web site hosting together with merchant capabilities. In the discussion below we will assume that there is a Web site available to assist with producing reasonable merchant capabilities, although as mentioned, some selling capabilities are possible with a blog alone.

Shopping Carts and Merchant Accounts

An electronic shopping cart is the online equivalent of a physical shopping cart. Products will have some sort of "add to cart" button that adds items to the shopping cart, and when users are done shopping, the shopping cart automatically calculates and totals orders. Most shopping cart software also accepts payment information, for example credit card details, but does not actually process them.

To process credit cards, you need a merchant account, preferably one that interfaces with your shopping cart so that you have real-time credit card processing. A merchant account will charge setup fees, monthly fees, gateway fees, a flat fee per transaction plus a percentage fee per transaction, and perhaps additional fees. Many different merchant accounts are available. Some are more cost efficient for handling small numbers of orders whereas others are designed and priced for merchants who have a large volume of orders.

In the end, you can get a state-of-the-art shopping cart which has all the functionality you need, including many things we haven't even touched on here, plus a merchant account, for approximately $500 to $1,000 a year. This doesn't include the per transaction fees which range from approximately 15 cents to 50 cents per transaction plus 2 percent to 3.5 percent.

Shopping Cart Choices

You could have a custom shopping cart built. It could either be extremely simple, or complex and full featured.

A simple example could use a form to allow users to check off what they want to buy and enter credit card or other payment information. A form is simple, but without a lot of custom programming, it won't be able to do many desirable things, such as calculate shipping (regular or priority, for example); calculate tax, if any; create and track associate links; automatically send confirmation e-mails; store customer information; encrypt payment information for protection and privacy; actually invoke the credit card processing; etc.

A fully featured shopping cart takes a lot of time and custom programming to build, and unless the designers and programmers have a lot of experience in this area, it usually makes sense to use an established one. It certainly is possible to create your own, just as some people build their own blogging software, but uncommon.

Another shopping cart option is PayPal. PayPal has its own simple shopping cart or it can be integrated into other shopping carts, and it processes credit cards and other payments. PayPal does not require a separate merchant account, which makes it ideal for many businesses. PayPal also has simple "buy now" buttons for single item sales that can be used instead of a shopping cart. PayPal transfers the customer to its Web site to complete payment, which is unacceptable or undesirable for many. PayPal also has a new Web site Payments Pro option with limited availability, which does not transfer customers to its Web site to complete payment.

SUMMARY

Blog readers are a prequalified group to which you can market. Many of them presumably have some connection to or overlap of interests with the blogger or their organization, and probably include current and potential customers. However, explicitly earning money may or may not be in line with a blog's primary purpose, such as customer communications, support, marketing, or internal communications, among others. When explicitly earning money is not an option, implicit methods may be acceptable and even desirable. It is important that the blog not turn into a blog-equivalent of a poor late-night infomercial, but that it retain its authenticity and honesty in order to be effective!

In the next few chapters, we'll talk about planning, creating, and promoting your blog, as well as how to measure its effectiveness.

Chapter

7

PLANNING YOUR BLOG

In the Andy Hardy movies of the 1940s,
Mickey Rooney and Judy Garland found themselves faced with a
dilemma, usually along the lines of a heartless bank ready to fore-
close on grandpa's farm. In a split second of inspiration, one of
them would say, "I know! Let's put on a show!" And with nary a
complication, the pair would produce a Broadway-quality show in
grandpa's barn and save the day.

Such last-minute innovation worked for Andy Hardy. It will
not work for a business blog. Your business blog should be ap-
proached as any other business communication: strategically.

Strategy is a word businesses bandy about with reckless
abandon. We apply the simplest definition of the term. Your blog
will be strategic if it is planned and implemented to help the business achieve its business goals. "We need a blog because our competitor has a blog" is not a strategic approach to blogging (or any
other kind of organizational communication, for that matter).
What if your competitor produced a video? Would you respond,

"Our competitor has a video, so we need a video. I don't know what it will be about or who we'll show it to, but they have one, by God, so we're going to have one, too!"

Nor should you blog because business publications tell you that you should. Paying attention to business coverage of blogging is a good idea, but blogging should respond to your own unique business issues and needs. Identifying those issues and needs is the heart of strategic communication.

LISTEN

The first step to take when planning a business blog is to stop. Take a deep breath. And start to read. While the act in which you engage will be reading, your real goal at this stage is to *listen*. Listen to the issues that bloggers and those posting comments are raising. Listen to the tone. Listen to the ebb and flow of conversation and how readers and bloggers react to one another and their posts.

Blogging is not an activity undertaken in a vacuum. As we have stated consistently throughout this book—and as we will continue to reiterate in chapters to come—blogging is a conversation. If you view your corporate blogs as a means by which you can push a message out to an audience, kind of like a column published in a marketing magazine, you are likely to experience some surprising repercussions as those already part of this global conversation start talking about you; and it won't be pretty. You need to get a sense of how the blogosphere works and you need to get into the habit of listening. If you're not inclined to listen—to those who comment on your blog, to others blogging on the same subjects, to bloggers who post items about what you have written—then don't blog. Find another way to get your message out. There are plenty of options. Blogging is every bit as much about *listening* as it is about *posting*.

Savvy business leaders already recognize the value of listening. Conventional wisdom suggests that customer complaints represent your best source of information you can use to make your business more competitive and successful. Your blog will undoubtedly attract its fair share of complaints. You'll also hear recommendations, ideas, competitive intelligence, consumer preferences—all manner of input that could inform your decision making if you are able to filter it and identify the bits that would lead to better products, customer relations, and decision making.

FOCUS

Employing a strategic approach to business blogging presumes that you have started with a goal and worked your way through strategies and objectives. While an individual might start a blog as a channel for talking about whatever he or she feels like talking about, your business blog needs to focus on subject matter aligned with the goals you are trying to achieve.

This does not mean, of course, that once you launch your strategically focused blog that it is not a candid, authentic, authoritative channel for communicating with your audience. It simply means that the blog will not deviate from its theme. Cisco Systems, for example, has a public blog dedicated to high-tech policy. The blog's home page proclaims, "(Worldwide Government Affairs) started this blog in an effort to share the public policy expertise and opinions of our team members." Imagine if one of the government affairs bloggers decided to comment on, say, quarterly earnings or new product plans. Readers who subscribe to the blog will stop reading as fewer posts deal with government policy, and the effort to promote and discuss Cisco's perspectives on high-tech policy will be diluted.

What happens when you *don't* select a strategy-driven theme? The CEO of iFulfill.com, an Ohio-based Internet fulfillment company, launched a blog in May 2005 focusing on his personal interest: work-life balance. At the same time, his company was going under. Unhappy customers began using the comment section of the blog to express their dismay and anger while competitors posted comments offering their services.

Many believe that the CEO would have been better served launching a blog to discuss the state of the business, to candidly address the issues the company was facing, and to engage in a conversation with his key stakeholders about how to fix it. Alternatively, he could have launched no blog at all. But to start a blog designed to attract customers based on the fact that the CEO is a nice guy with strong values was misguided, to say the least.

Other examples of blogs that stay focused on specific themes include the following.

- GM's FastLane blog is about cars. There is no discussion of business issues such as labor or financial performance, despite ongoing pressure to discuss these issues in the blog. GM is more interested in engaging in a conversation with the car-buying public about what they want in a vehicle, though, and it continues to address other issues using alternative communication media.
- EDS's fellows—a title awarded to the company's thought leaders—author the Next Big Thing blog, which stays focused on the future of technology. As with GM, there is no discussion of other business issues.
- The Wharton business school at the University of Pennsylvania maintains MBA Admissions Blog, which deals with issues relevant to MBA applicants as they prepare to apply to business schools.
- AARP's Issues Blog reports on issues that are important to the lobbying group's constituency, such as Social Security and health care. Not addressed: membership issues, finances, and the like.

- Boeing's Flight Test Journal allows test pilots to report on their experiences testing a new model of the airplane manufacturer's 777 aircraft. Other planes, finances, labor, and any topic other than flight-testing the 777-200LR are considered strictly off topic.

How do you decide the focus of your blog? It will depend entirely on the conditions and circumstances of your business. They key is to focus on business, not blogging. "I want to have a blog; what should it be about?" is not the approach to take. Instead, recognize that you have an issue and you need to engage in a conversation with your customers about it; then determine how you should go about it, A blog may well present itself as the solution.

While this approach lends itself to virtually every public blog you might want to launch, it does *not* apply to any employee blogging programs you may introduce. Under these programs (as discussed in Chapter 2), employees author their own blogs, serving as representatives of the organization and talking about their own work and the focus of their own efforts. The focus of their blogs is the passion an individual employee blogger has for his or her area of expertise combined with the expertise itself. In this case, you still need to know why you're introducing employee blogs. IBM had two reasons for introducing employee blogging: to evangelize IBM product and to see what the company could learn from the exercise that would be applicable to future efforts. Microsoft wanted the public to see that the company was made up of dedicated, enthusiastic employees who cared about the quality of the work they produced. Thomas Nelson Publishers CEO Michael Hyatt articulated three reasons for wanting his employees to blog publicly:

1. Raise the visibility of the company and its products.
2. Make a contribution to the publishing community.
3. Give people a look at what goes on inside a real publishing company.

Understanding these goals will help employees keep their blogs focused on accomplishing them, regardless of what the theme of each individual blog may be.

WHO SHOULD BLOG?

For each blog your company produces, you'll need to decide who the author or authors should be. For example, a CEO enthusiastic about the potential benefits of blogging may be anxious to undertake the authorship of the blog himself. But for various reasons, he may not be the best person to pen the blog. He may have a stilted writing style. Perhaps he would be more of a target for inappropriate comments than another executive. In the case of Sun Microsystems, CEO Scott McNealy does not have a blog. Sun's highest ranking blogger is Jonathan Schwartz, the company's president and chief operating officer. As a high-tech company, having Schwartz write the senior-most blog keeps the focus on technology instead of business decisions.

In some organizations, writers are hired specifically to write blogs; in others, blogging is one of the job requirements. Stonyfield Farms, for example, hired Christine Halvorson, a former journalist and almanac writer, to pen the dairy's blog, The Bovine Bugle. She writes in her own voice, never pretending to be anything or anyone that she isn't. She is the official company blogger; in fact, her job title is chief blogger.

Not all companies will hire a blogger, nor is it always a good idea. Halvorson's job is to build an emotional connection between consumers and the company. Other blogs have different goals. For example, a blog by a subject matter expert puts the company's thought leadership on display. One by a technician keeps readers up to date on the maintenance of a complex system. A blog by a technical support representative helps customers with their own tech support issues, precluding the need to call in to the company's tech support line. In other words, in addition to being passionate about the subject matter and an engaging writer, the blogger should be an expert in the subject matter pertaining to the blog.

In each of these cases, the blogger is the best person to discuss the issues at hand. But the task requires certain other traits and characteristics. Any employee undertaking a blog should have the following characteristics:

- The ability to write in a natural, authentic, human voice
- The time to dedicate to posting items at least a couple times a week
- The time to monitor comments and read other related blogs
- The skills required to listen to comments and shape the blog into a conversation with readers
- The commitment to stick with the blog

A final consideration as you decide whom your blogger should be is whether you'll have only one blogger writing for any given blog. There are plenty of group blogs out there in which multiple authors contribute. The best known example is the General Motors FastLane blog. While GM vice chairman Bob Lutz is the most frequent of the FastLane bloggers, he is routinely joined by other senior GM executives, including Bryan Nesbitt, executive director of GM Europe design; Robert Lange, executive director of structure and safety integration; and Tom Kowaleski, vice president, communications. In each case, these executive authors apply their expertise about the theme of the blog: cars.

The primary advantage of a group blog should be obvious: it absolves any one blogger of the responsibility to post frequently. As long as each blogger posts with some regularity, the blog will be updated with plenty of fresh content. This approach also provides a diversity of voices and ensures that the best person to talk about a specific issue is posting based on his or her area of expertise.

The disadvantage of a group blog should be equally obvious: the single, authentic, human voice is diluted by a plurality of voices. You'll have to decide if the advantages outweigh the disadvantages if you're considering a group blog.

There is one last class of blog authors worth talking about before we move on. Known alternately as character blogs or fake blogs, the true author of these blogs is never really known. That's just as well because, if history provides any insight, the true author would be the subject of intense derision.

A character blog is one that is ostensibly written by a fictional character. One of the most notorious examples of a character blog came from Captain Morgan rum, in which Captain Morgan—the red-suited pirate—"wrote" the blog. It was generally blasted as lame and insipid, and it didn't last long.

Other character blogs have been even worse and have suffered the same barrage of insults from the blogosphere. Steve Rubel, the A-list public relations blogger (and author of the Micro Persuasion blog) wrote in mid-2005: "Character blogs are a waste of time because a character is not and never will be human . . . I am all for using characters in TV commercials and even micro-sites, but having them blog is just a lame, lazy idea. In fact, it's an insult to blogging and bloggers everywhere . . . (companies behind character blogs) haven't studied it enough to know that blogging is a conversation. It's about being real and transparent. The good news is that if advertisers continue to play ignorant, the lionshare (sic) of corporate blog dollars will flow into the PR industry because we get it. I can sleep easier at night knowing that Captain Morgan and other characters are blogging."

It's not unthinkable that a decent character blog may someday emerge. Shel has noted on his blog that if Cartman, the super-sized character from the *South Park,* ever starts a blog, he'll read it as long as it's funny, untroubled by the fact that it is neither authentic nor an opportunity to engage in a conversation. But even this idea is a very limited one that could not be duplicated for corporate use. While someday an organization may produce a popular and highly lauded character blog, your best bet is to avoid character blogs at all costs.

SOME GUIDELINES FOR SUCCESSFUL BLOGS

Blogs that genuinely help the organization meet its goals have characteristics in common. Following are some guidelines that can be gleaned from the behaviors of bloggers producing these most effective blogs:

Dos

- Read a lot of other blogs. You are part of a community of bloggers; you are not communicating in a vacuum.
- Write passionately about your company and its products or services. If you are not a true believer, why are you blogging on your company's behalf?
- Put other employees on display. Conduct interviews with other passionate workers who don't have a blog but whose insights are relevant to the theme of your own blog.
- Focus your blog on a theme and an audience.
- Keep posts short, for the most part. Longer, analytical posts are acceptable now and then, but not on a regular basis. Under 1,000 words is a good goal.
- Link. Linking is at the heart of blogging.

Don'ts

- Pitch product or sales in your blog. That's what advertising is for. Readers will turn off instantly if they find themselves being pitched.

- Post in haste. You may regret what you've written if you don't take the time to review it carefully, particularly if you are responding to criticism or fast-breaking events.

Editing, Review, and Approval

Most content produced in a company that will be seen by the public goes through a review-and-approval process. Everything from press releases to marketing brochures, earnings statements to executive speeches, is vetted by lawyers, PR staff, and a variety of other in-house overseers.

In general, your blogs should be excluded from this process. Instead of *reactively* reviewing blogs to ensure their content won't cause problems outside the organization, you should *proactively* ensure that your bloggers know the limitations of what they can and cannot say. The best way to do this is to develop and communicate a blogging policy. (Elements of policies are covered in Chapter 6.)

If this seems risky, the risk is minimized if you trust your employees and thoroughly communicate their obligations and responsibilities while blogging. The benefit is content that doesn't sound forced, artificial, filtered, or edited, which is exactly what customers and other audiences expect from a blog. Or, as Sun Microsystems chief technology evangelist Simon Phipps put it in an interview with *Technology Review,* "In a world where you must speak with an authentic voice, the obvious way is to let the people you most trust—your employees—speak directly to the people you most want to appeal to—your customers."

Besides, what attorney would want to review every post to every official company blog, particularly if hundreds or thousands of employees are blogging?

In addition to ensuring posts are free of the kind of "corporatese" that seeps into copy that is filtered through attorneys and communications professionals, avoiding the review-and-approval process also helps get the posts up in the most timely possible manner, which can be particularly important when a conversation has emerged on the blog between the employee author and the audience of readers. Conversations that take place in as close to real time as possible are far more effective than those in which comments are delayed while they are routed through the approval process.

Of course, there may be instances when the content of blog posts simply demands that it be reviewed by an attorney or some other authority (such as the head of investor relations, a regulatory affairs specialist, or a product manager). How do you ensure these posts get the stamp of approval they need while keeping the rest off your counsel's plate? Simple. Your policies should include a concise list of the issues and subjects that require approval, along with a roster of the right authority to contact. And again, you'll need to start trusting your employees to take the appropriate action when considering such a post.

Design Considerations

Planning a business blog should also include some thinking about what the blog should look like. Most blogging applications come with a fair number of templates you can choose, and several of the platforms, including WordPress and Expression Engine, boast communities of individuals who seem to think creating new design templates is the height of entertainment, leaving a wealth of design alternatives available for you to download.

For your business blog, however, you should look at a unique design that integrates the design standards established for your company's corporate brand (or the product brand, if the blog focuses on a product). The design should also reflect the character of the blog: Is it businesslike? Fun? Issues-oriented?

Controversial? The blog should help reinforce that personality. At the very least, you'll want to ensure appropriate logos and color schemes are reflected on the blog. Make sure the design is replicated on all the various templates; not just the home page, but also the comments and category pages, for example.

Creating such templates will require the services of somebody who understands online design, but it will also need to retain the tags that drive the blog. Tags are established by the developer of the blog platform and ensure various elements—posts, trackbacks, comments, etc.—all appear where and how they should.

The actual work of revising the design, though, is usually just a matter of making changes to an existing template rather than developing one from scratch.

What about the design of your employee blogs? In this case, you can provide employees with a number of templates from which to choose, then allow them to modify those templates to reflect their own personalities (within reason, of course). In some organizations, employee blogs are not hosted on the company's servers. Instead, employees are encouraged to create blogs using the service of their choice and then inform the company of its URL so a comprehensive list of employee blogs can be offered. In this case, design is entirely up to the employees who create blogs.

Comments

How you will handle comments is among the most important decisions to make. Comments drive the conversation; you will do you most active listening when reading comments and deciding how to act on those that demand action.

Your first decision, of course, is whether you should open the blog to comments at all. To be sure, there are many corporate blogs that don't accept comments. Boeing vice president Randy Baesler, for example, will post comments he gets via e-mail and other channels, but leaves the commenting feature of the blog inactive. In response to criticism that he isn't allowing comments in contravention of widely accepted blogging guidelines, Baesler wrote, "I didn't realize that the blogosphere had such a rule. Sorry, that's just not what we're about. Sure, we're going to post some of your comments. Even critical ones. But it's not a free-for-all."

GM's Bob Lutz disagrees. Writing in *Information Week* about his blogging experiences, the automaker's vice chairman wrote, "Another aspect that helps keep things real is the wealth of comments posted by readers and other bloggers. We don't filter out negative comments, complaints, or hate mail. All we do is screen for spam and posts from crackpots using language that most people would find offensive.

"It's important that we run the bad with the good. We'd take a credibility hit if we posted only rosy compliments, and credibility is the most important attribute a corporate blog can have. Once it's gone, your blog is meaningless.

"If you filter the negatives out, you don't have a true dialogue, so how can you hope to change anybody's mind about your products or your business? And changing minds is priority one at GM."

Lutz has it exactly right. If blogging is about establishing a dialogue with your audience—a conversation with customers—you have to be prepared for that conversation to take whatever turns it might. You need to grow a thick skin and be ready to hear criticisms and treat your critics with respect while taking their comments seriously. Once again, if you're not prepared to hear the bad along with the good, don't blog.

So we think it is best that you enable commenting on your blog. Your policy will allow for the harshest criticism as well as the highest praise. You may feel free, as General Motors did, to insist that comments be free of the foul language that would offend (as the lawyers like to say) a reasonable person. Next, you need to consider whether your blog's comment section will be moderated. Moderation means that comments are queued up for your review.

Only after you have read and approved them are they published to the post where the public can see them.

Comment moderation is a judgment call. If you can ensure the comments will be reviewed frequently and posted quickly, there's no harm in checking to make sure all comments comply with your published guidelines. On the other hand, a reader who posts a comment and waits hours (or even days) to see it will be turned off by the blog and its apparent lack of commitment to dialogue. It's easy to remove offensive posts reactively, and the benefit you accrue by letting legitimate comments appear as soon as they are submitted—and that represents the vast majority of the comments you'll get—could easily outweigh the risk of having an offensive post on the blog for an hour or two.

Comment spam represents one last reason to consider comment moderation. It's the main reason individual bloggers moderate comments. It's not that they want to screen what legitimate readers have to say, but rather than they want to filter out illegitimate comments that are really designed just to boost the visibility of a product or service, such as mortgages, poker rooms, online pharmacies, and the like. Some of these comments are blatant, loaded with references to the advertised product, while others are subtle, including comments like, "Very interesting post; you shed light on this topic." The signature, though, links to the advertising site.

There are other ways to deal with comment spam, such as CAPTCHA, which requires readers to enter a word they see displayed as a graphic. This will stop automated comment spam, but not a dedicated comment spammer who is manually visiting blogs and posting comments one at a time. (CAPTCHA also precludes a visually impaired visitor from commenting on your posts.)

Next, you'll need to decide whether you or your other bloggers will respond directly to comments. Unlike message boards (also known as bulletin boards and forums), there is no expectation among those posting comments that you will reply to their input. On the other hand, there *is* an expectation that you won't ignore them! How do you reconcile these seemingly irreconcilable sets of expectations?

First, you could decide to respond directly to a comment by adding your own comment. Yep, that's right. You can comment in your own blog to a comment offered to your own post. In fact, it's not an uncommon practice. Depending on the level and nature of your blog, you will need to consider whether you will engage in such a direct dialogue and to what level. For example, a customer service–focused blog might include a rich dialogue between blogger and audience. On the other hand, a CEO blogger would want to be far more judicious in selecting the comments that cry out for a one-to-one reply. Some executive bloggers opt never to reply directly to a comment, instead crafting a new post that reads something like this: "A number of you had some interesting observations in your comments to my post on our new product line. Thanks for your candid thoughts! Here's what I heard . . ."

Whatever approach you take, you should be consistent. Beyond the exception when you feel a direct response to a comment is required, if you're going to respond to comments, you should do so regularly. And you should always remember that the nature of the blog is conversational, so you should adopt one of these approaches and never ignore the comments you receive.

SUMMARY

If you leap without looking into the blogosphere, you'll suffer the consequences, which can be serious. On the other hand, your chances of creating a successful blog increase if you plan your blogging efforts so they are aligned with your business goals, issues, and strategies.

The same approach should be taken when implementing blogs on your intranet. (Intranet blogs are covered in Chapter 3.)

8

HOW TO CREATE A BLOG—
STEP-BY-STEP

Blogs and Web sites can be manually cre-
ated in the hypertext markup language (HTML) using a simple
text editor, just as a carpenter could cut down trees and make his
own lumber. Obviously few bloggers, Webmasters, or carpenters
take this approach because it is too time consuming and there is
too much room for error.

Most Web sites are created with special purpose software designed specifically for creating a Web site, such as Microsoft Frontpage or Macromedia Dreamweaver. Web site software can be used
to create blogs as well, although it is difficult because it is not designed with blogs in mind. The vast majority of blogs are created
and updated with special purpose blogging software. Fortunately,
there are several different options available today, and each one
has its distinct advantages and disadvantages.

If you will not be actually setting up and maintaining a blog
you can skip this chapter. Many bloggers have their blogs created
and maintained by others, so they can concentrate on writing the

content. However, if you'll be setting up or maintaining your own blog or you're even mildly interested in how it's done, this chapter shows just how easy it is.

BLOGGING SOFTWARE

There are a lot of choices when it comes to choosing blogging software. They range from a number of free choices, such as Blogger and LiveJournal (which include free blog hosting), and Wordpress (which can be downloaded and installed for free); choices with monthly fees, such as TypePad; and software for outright purchase such as Movable Type. Not all choices are discussed here, but we've attempted to cover many of the most popular and those most likely to be in existence for a while. Blogging software is evolving fairly rapidly so contact the vendors for up-to-the-minute details of features and functionality.

Hosted versus Nonhosted Solutions

There are two choices in types of blogging software, hosted and nonhosted solutions. With a hosted solution, the software and the data, blog posts, comments, etc., reside on the blogging software company's server. With a nonhosted solution, the software needs to be downloaded and installed on a server owned or leased by the organization, and the data will reside on the organization's server as well.

Hosted solutions are simpler because there is nothing to install. Often an aspiring blogger can literally be up and blogging in a manner of minutes. Many hosted solutions are less flexible because you don't control the software or hardware; you simply access it over the Internet. There are some drawbacks to hosted services you should consider. For example, the blogging company might go out of business, stop hosting blogs, or financial or other circumstances might make them unreliable. Weblogs.com, a pioneer Web logging service, suddenly closed down its Web hosting in June 2004, stranding perhaps thousands of bloggers and blogs.

Hosted solutions are often ideal for employee blogs at organizations where the organization is not providing blogging software or Web site space for blogs, for example Microsoft and Thomas Nelson Publishers. Hosted solutions are also ideal for organizations that do not have a Web site—yes, they still exist—or that want their employee blogs somehow separated from the organization's home site.

With a nonhosted solution, the blogging software and blogs reside on the organization's servers. Many organizations require full control of all their data, including their Web sites and their blogs, and a nonhosted solution allows this. This may be their standard operating procedure, and may be required by their information security or other policy. Required control may include how often information is backed up and how backups are done, the type of hardware on which sites and blogs are hosted, and how much effort is spent on robustness, security solutions, etc. The only way to have full control is to have the blogging software and blogs on machines physically controlled by the organization (i.e., a non-hosted solution).

With a hosted solution, your blog is associated with the hosting company's brand. For example, the Blogger.com terms of service require you to display a Blogger.com graphic on your blog. In some cases, the content might not even be legally yours; you need to check the agreements carefully.

With a hosted solution, the URL or Internet name for your blog will usually reference the blogger software provider's domain. For example, a blog's URL might be thetedrap.blogspot.com, livejournal.com/users/thetedrap, or thetedrap.typepad.com. These are the URLs Ted's blog, The Ted Rap, would have if it were on the hosted services Blogger, LiveJournal, and TypePad, respectively.

Many organizations want their blog to promote and extend their brand, and not necessarily be associated with the name of the hosting service. Alternatively, some organizations simply do not have an issue with this.

There is a third choice besides hosting the blog on the organization's domain or hosting it under the blogging software hosting solutions domain. An organization could decide to host its blogs under a domain it operates other than its main domain. For example, Organization XYZ, with a main Web site at xyz.com, could decide to host its blogs under xyzblogs.com. The blogs are clearly under the organization's control and brand, yet there is some level of separation between the main Web site and the blog or blogs; between the formal corporate Web site and the more personal, informal, and conversational writing of the blog or blogs.

Some hosted blogging services support domain forwarding, which allows pointing a registered domain name or subdomain name to the blog's hosted URL. For example, a blog hosted by Type-Pad may have a URL of myblog.typepad.com, but with domain forwarding, the world will access the blog under a different domain name. This will allow a domain or subdomain you own, such as example.com or blog.example.com, to point to a TypePad blog such as example.typepad.com. This allows visitors to access your blog via your domain or subdomain name, and never see the hosted URL.

Some nonhosted blog solutions are supported by Internet hosting providers. In this case, an organization can lease a Web server and installed blogging software, which will reside on the hosting provider's premises. What's the difference between a hosted blog solution such as Blogger or LiveJournal and a nonhosted solution such as Movable Type where support is purchased from a hosting provider? It's actually quite simple. A hosted blog solution provides space for hosting only blogs. A hosting provider who supports a nonhosted blogging software solution will provide space for blogs and other material; for example, your entire corporate Web site.

Hosted blogs. Hosted blogs are incredibly simple to set up. There is no software to install or configure. There are no concerns as to whether your server supports the blogging software as it's run on the hosting company's servers and typically accessed via your browser. An aspiring blogger simply creates an account, picks a basic blog design, and starts blogging. The basic blog design, usually called a template, can also be personalized and customized later as desired.

Blogger may be the most popular blogging service available. A Blogger.com blog can be created and up and running in a few minutes, and is entirely free, which contributes to its popularity immensely. Blogger blogs are hosted at blogspot.com by default, with a URL format of http://myblogname.blogspot.com. Blogger also supports an option to publish your blog at any URL you wish. For example, Ted uses Blogger but his blog resides at http://www.demop.com/thetedrap.

Blogger does not support some blog features that lots of other blogging software does, most notably categories and trackbacks. Blogger also doesn't support RSS feeds, although it supports the rival Atom format. Free add-ons are available to support trackbacks as well as several other features, and although we know of no add-ons to support categories, they can be implemented fairly simply on a blog-by-blog case. In the words of Blogger, "We do not yet have a way to import posts from other blogging tools." Some popular free add-ons include enhanced blogroll capability from BlogRolling.com, enhanced commenting and trackbacks from Haloscan.com, and free e-mail interfaces from Feedblitz.com, BotABlog.com, and others.

Google purchased Blogger in February 2003, and many Blogger users expect Google will enhance and extend Blogger to include missing features. Ted currently uses Blogger, and the few times he considered switching to another service because of a needed but missing feature, Blogger seemed to suddenly implement it or an add-on became available from a third party.

It is worth noting that some bloggers are prejudiced against Blogger blogs, just as there is some prejudice against Internet users with an e-mail address "@aol.com." Both are sometimes considered to be marks of new and unsophisticated users, and Blogger.com also has a proliferation of spam blogs.

LiveJournal is a very popular blogging package built on open source software, used by over eight million blogs. It is quite simple to use, although it has limited customization features. Both free accounts and very inexpensive paid accounts (currently $19.95 a year) are available. Paid accounts offer additional features including domain forwarding. The standard URL for a LiveJournal blog has the format http://www.livejournal.com/users/myblogname/. LiveJournal has some interesting social networking features as well.

Although LiveJournal blogs on the whole are more "personal journal" or "diary" type blogs, LiveJournal is used for a number of intranet blogs.

Six Apart, which also owns TypePad and Moveable Type, purchased LiveJournal in January 2005.

TypePad is a full-featured and extremely popular blogging package, and is available in basic, plus, and pro levels of service, which run between $4.95 and $14.95 a month with discounts by the year. The basic level allows one blog for one author, and is so simple that it can be set up in minutes, somewhat like Blogger. There are a number of blog templates or looks that can be chosen. The plus level allows up to three blogs for one author and gives you more control over what your blog looks like via the TypePad template builder. The pro level allows unlimited blogs and multiple authors, along with direct access to all HTML code so that blogs are fully customizable.

TypePad blogs are hosted at typepad.com, and URLs have the format http://www.myblogname.typepad.com. The plus and pro levels support domain forwarding, which TypePad refers to as domain mapping.

TypePad supports importing contents from other blogs, and includes specific instructions for Blogger, Moveable Type, and Radio UserLand, as well as exporting contents.

Radio UserLand is unique in that blogs are created locally by software that is downloaded and installed on the client, and then uploaded to the Web server. This allows updating blogs while offline, which is useful, but requires a specially configured machine for updating blogs. It is supported on Windows as well as Macintosh, and English, Italian, and French versions are available. It takes only minutes to create a blog with Radio UserLand. Blogs can be hosted on Radio UserLand's site or a site of your choice. Radio UserLand costs $39.95 yearly.

Radio UserLand includes a bundled RSS feedreader, and easily facilitates commenting on current news items. There are directions for importing from Blogger and Movable Type. It has the capability to create special pages for important information or for unusually long posts. Features of advanced outline processing markup language (OPML), a collaborative outlining tool, are available, but details are beyond the scope of this book. John Udell describes them as well as anyone in an article that can be found at http://www.oreillynet.com/lpt/a/webservices/2002/04/01/outlining.html.

Nonhosted solutions. Nonhosted solutions consist of blogging software that needs to be installed on your own server. Note that many generic Web site hosting providers may not support the necessary software to host all blogging solutions. For example, many require a MySQL database, and some hosting providers do not provide MySQL support. Also, some hosting providers explicitly may disallow the use of specific software due to processor load and other concerns. If using a hosting provider, always check to see if it supports any blogging solution you are considering to avoid any misunderstandings. For example, Ted uses a well-known and established hosting provider for his company's Web site, but it does not support any of the nonhosted solutions listed below!

Movable Type is extremely similar to, but not exactly the same as, TypePad because they are based on the same codebase. It is one of the best-known blogging software packages, and it is extremely popular, powerful, and flexible. It has the reputation of being somewhat hard to install and use for nontechnical people. Movable Type has many different versions available: several "personal" versions, including a free unsupported one; and several commercial, educational, and not-for-profit versions.

It runs on several operating systems including Windows Server, various Unix platforms, including Linux, and Mac OS X; and it supports many Web servers and databases. Check the Web site to confirm that it can run on your Web server platform. Movable Type hosting is available from several hosting providers for those who do not want to install or support the Movable Type software.

PMachines' **ExpressionEngine** is an impressive package that is much more flexible and includes far more functionality than a pure blogging package. It could be described more accurately as a content management system that handles blogs extremely well. It includes functionality not normally associated with blogging software: workflow features that allow the user to define file status (e.g., draft, pending, final edit, etc.) to allow multiple authors to contribute to content; double opt-in mailing list functionality; and photo-editing features like image cropping, resizing, and thumbnailing. The community of ExpressionEngine users has created numerous plug-ins and templates. ExpressionEngine runs on most platforms that support the MySQL database; see the PMachines Web site for full details.

Greymatter is an open source blogging package by Noah Grey that is fully customizable and "tweakable." It is intended as a flexible power tool for those comfortable with HTML. Unlike most blogging software, it does not require a database to be installed on the host system. About the only requirement for running Greymatter is the Perl language version 5, which is free software that runs on most systems.

Web hosting company Plug Socket offers hosting packages that include bundled Greymatter support. Greymatter is no longer being actively developed by Noah Grey, although there is a significant support community. It is not suitable for most organizations for business blogging purposes.

WordPress is a very popular and free open source blogging package, which is stable, full-featured, and extensible. In tune with its open source heritage, there are hundreds of free software plug-ins and extensions available, as well as an active support community. Importers are available for Movable Type, Greymatter, Blogger, and others. WordPress runs on most platforms that support the MySQL database and PHP, a widely available and popular open source programming language.

A number of hosting companies offer WordPress support, and WordPress has recently starting a free hosting service.

Switching Blog Software

It is possible, with some difficulty, to switch your blogging software once your blog is established. It is also possible to move a blog's location, for example, from a common hosted space to your organization's server, again with some difficulty. It is not uncommon when switching blogging software to leave the old posts, links, comments, etc., behind at the old site and then start with new posts at the new site. Obviously this is not an ideal solution, but it is simple. It's also likely that if you move a blog's location, not all the readers will follow, regardless of how smoothly the move may go. When Ted moved his blog from http://www.thetedrap.blogspot.com to his company's Web site he lost more than half his readers and it took several months to build his audience back up.

Switching blogging software is difficult on many fronts. All the data (posts, comments, etc.) needs to be moved, and almost every type of blogging software has its own data format. Some blog software supports import/export routines, which help in this process. In the worst case, it is possible to copy and paste the posts individually, although this will result in losing any comments and trackbacks. As daunting as copying and pasting may seem, it sometimes may be the best option. If a blog is one year old, and has a post every weekday, that totals approximately 260 posts. Because many posts are on timely topics, it may make sense to move only a small portion of them. However, for a prolific or long-term blogger, the manual copy/paste option quickly becomes unworkable, unless the blogger only moves a select "best of" set of posts.

A related issue is that permalinks, the URL at which the blog posts are accessible after they scroll off the main page, vary depending on the blogger software. There is no standard. For example, compare the following permalinks:

- Blogger, http://<username>.blogspot.com/<4 digit year>/ <2 digit month>/<article name>.html
- WordPress, http://<site-specific prefix>/<4 digit year>/<2 digit month>/<2 digit date>/<article name>/
- Movable Type/TypePad, http://<username>.typepad.com/ <username>/<4 digit year>/<2 digit month>/<15 character name>.html

When switching blogging software, any links to the posts will become invalid. Search engines will need a while to reindex the entire blog. Any bookmarks users have saved to any of the blog posts will be invalid.

HOW TO CREATE A BLOG

We are going to look at an example of how to create a blog using Blogger.com. Creating the actual blog is fast and simple, and we'll also look at some simple customization, add-ons, and enhancements. Creating a blog with most other blog software will use many of the same concepts although they will differ somewhat.

The main Blogger.com page allows you to log in if you already have an account. It also allows you to take a quick tour of Blogger functionality, or create a blog. Click on the orange arrow that says "CREATE YOUR BLOG NOW." (See Figure 8.1.)

FIGURE 8.1 *Main Blogger.com Page*

Create Your Blog Now

Creating a blog is simple. You need to choose a username, which will be your login name. If you chose a name that has already been chosen, you will be asked to choose a different name when you click on the "CONTINUE" arrow. You need to choose a password of at least six characters and enter it twice. You are asked to enter it twice to make sure you get it right, especially because it doesn't echo on the screen as you type it. A display name is required. This is the name that is displayed after each post you make. Reading and accepting the terms of service is required before hitting the orange "CONTINUE" button. (See Figure 8.2.)

Next, you need to pick a title for your blog, as well as a blog address that will be of the form [yourblogname].blogspot.com by default. If you prefer, and have another place to host the blog, you can

FIGURE 8.2 *Creating a Blogger.com Account*

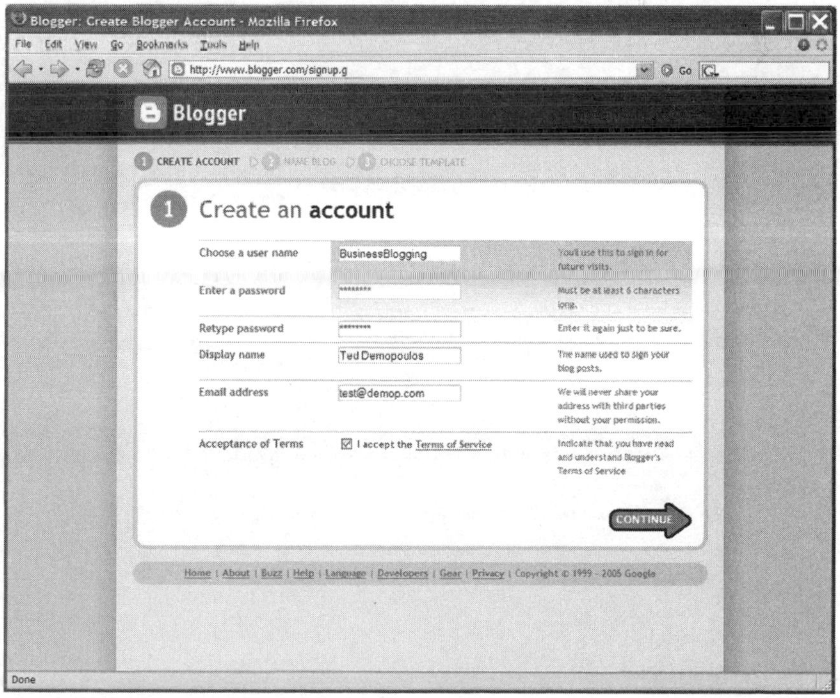

pick the "Advanced Setup" option. For example, Ted hosts his blog, The Ted Rap, at http://www.demop.com/thetedrap, a subdirectory of his company's Web site. We chose the blog title tedsbusinessblog as one word and a blog address of http://tedsbusinessblog .blogspot.com. These names are not required to be the same or related, although they are in this case. (See Figure 8.3.)

Note the word verification, or CAPTCHA as it is commonly called. This is used to prevent automated software robots from creating blogs. Most blogs created by automated software robots are spam blogs, also known as splogs. Splogs contain only spam posts, whose main purpose is to display a bunch of links for the

FIGURE 8.3 *Naming Your Blog*

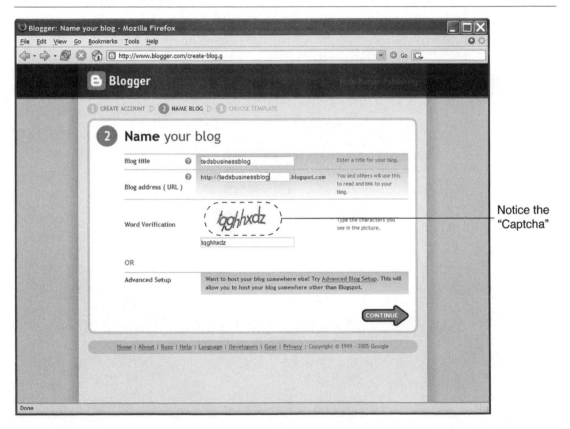

Notice the "Captcha"

search engines to find in order to boost the linked pages' apparent popularity. This is analogous to what spam comments attempt to do. Next, you need to choose a template, which defines the overall look and feel of your blog. Blogger offers 12 standard templates, and more can be found on the Internet. Templates can be and often are modified, and we will make some simple customizations to the template we choose. (See Figure 8.4.)

Choosing a template is similar to selecting a fax template in Microsoft Word. Most of the work is done for you, plus a few variables from Blogger's previous questions are automatically input for you so you're off and running!

FIGURE 8.4 *Choosing a Blog Template*

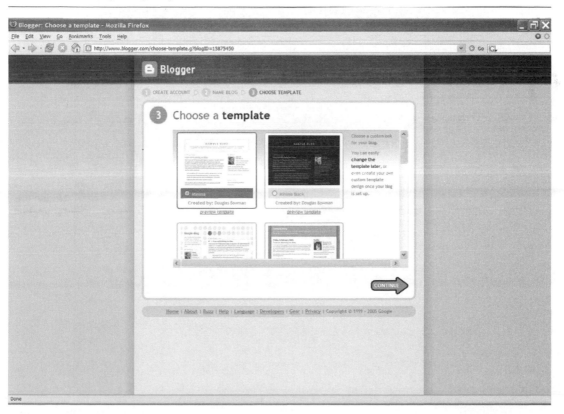

You can click on any template for a closer view. When we choose "Minima," the first template listed, it opens in a new window. (See Figure 8.5.)

We will use the Minima template (shown in Figure 8.5) and click the orange "CONTINUE" button.

Our blog is created. This took us only about ten minutes, and much of that time was spent looking at the various templates prior to choosing one. (See Figure 8.6.)

When we click on "Start Posting" we are immediately brought to the post editor. Because we're ready for an introductory post, we type in a title, "This is our First Post," and some text. The post editor is a very simple text editor. It allows us to compose either in text, or raw HTML if we prefer, and includes a "Preview" button that shows us exactly what our post will look like. The post

FIGURE 8.5 *The "Minima" Template*

FIGURE 8.6 *Your Blog Has Been Created!*

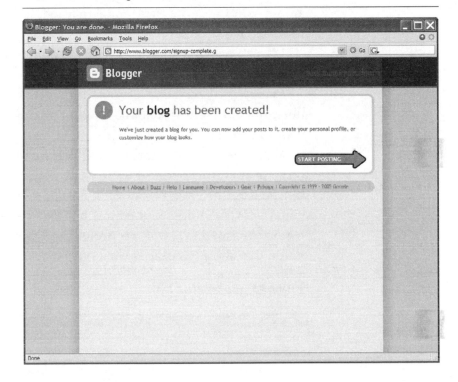

editor has a spell checker, and allows us to change the font, font size, and text color, as well as some other basic text editor functionality, without needing to directly access the HTML; it also allows us to add images and links to our posts. The "Recover post" button on the left-hand side allows recovering a post from a local temporary file if there was some error before the post was saved, such as the computer crashing. We can chose to allow or disallow comments on the post as well as modify the post date and time. Notice there is a help button in the upper right-hand corner in case we get confused. (See Figure 8.7.)

You will notice that there is an error in the text—an extra word ("very") in the last sentence. It is extremely difficult to proofread your own writing and sometimes errors do creep into blog posts. Although errors like this, as well as grammatical errors, typos,

FIGURE 8.7 *The Post Editor*

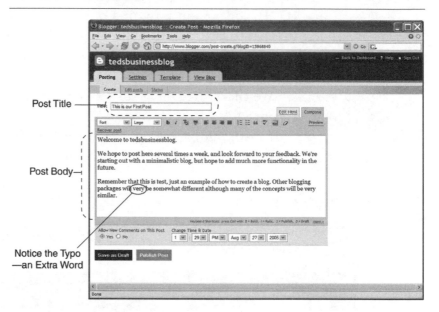

and others, often creep into blogs, do your best to minimize or eliminate them. Also note that although an error of this type in a formal communication such as a press release or corporate Web site would be almost unthinkable, it is not as critical in an "informal" medium such as a blog, although it is still quite undesirable. This extra word was corrected after the fact, despite the fact that the post was proofread twice before posting! Blogger easily lets you go back and edit any previous posts with the post editor. For example, when you first log in to Blogger and access your blog, it shows you the names of all your previous posts and allows you to edit any of them with a click of a button.

When we are done, we can publish the post which makes it visible on the blog, or save it as a draft, in which case it is not yet visible. Saving as a draft is very useful when you're not done writing, or want to proofread later or double check some facts referenced.

We chose to publish and a message informs us that the blog was published successfully. Sometimes this fails. Reasons may include that Blogger is down for service, there is illegal or corrupted HTML code in our post, or a number of other potential reasons. In the rare case that the publishing fails, we can simply retry again, correcting any problems such as illegal HTML code in our post. (See Figure 8.8.)

We click "View Blog" to see our blog for the first time. (See Figure 8.9.)

Here is our basic blog. Next we will add our picture and a few words about ourselves to the sidebar, and modify the links to

FIGURE 8.8 *Our Post Is Published*

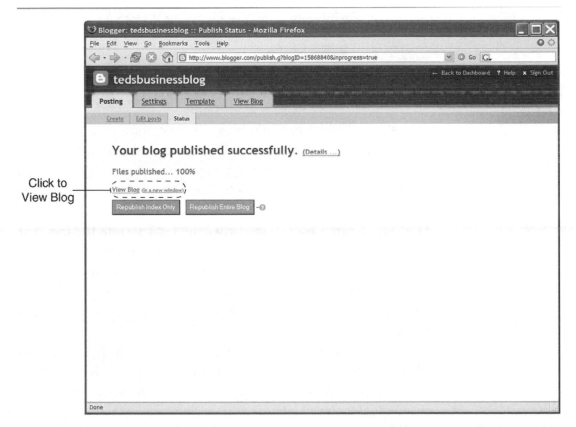

FIGURE 8.9 *Viewing Our Blog for the First Time*

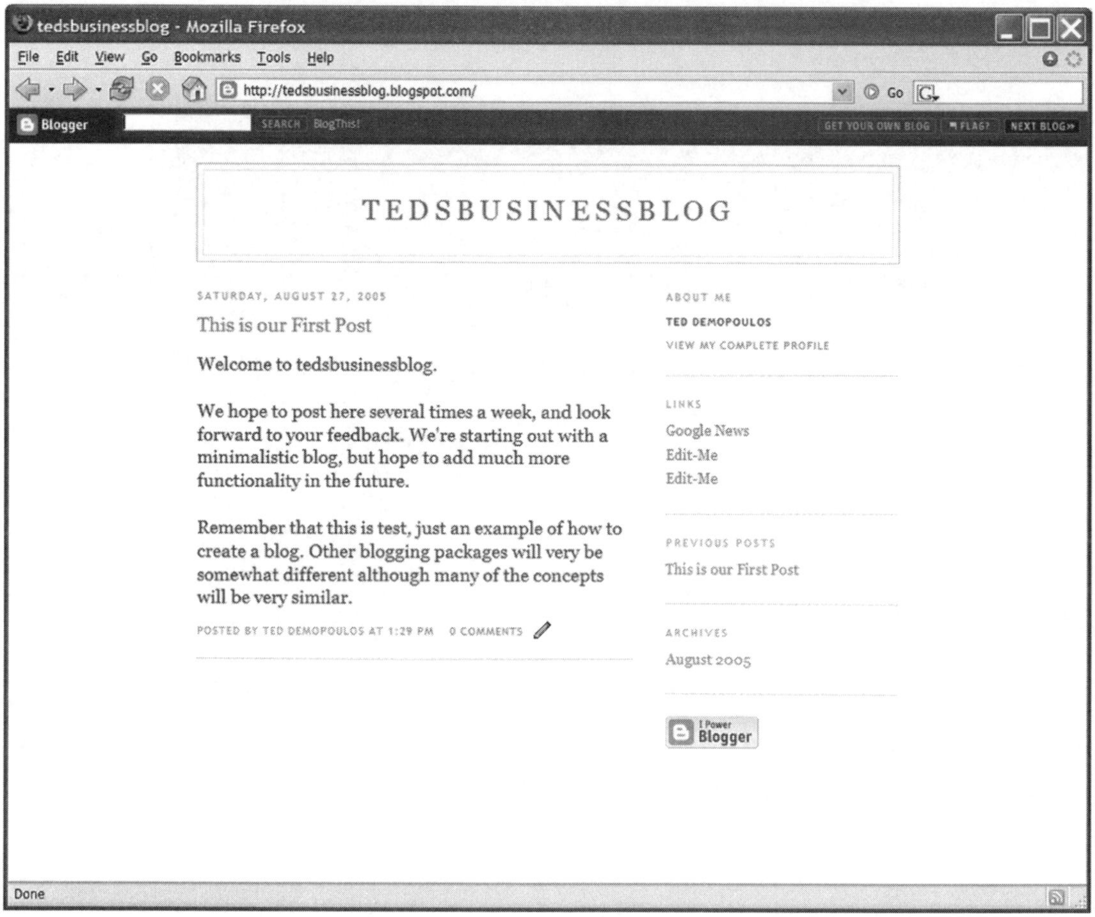

point to various places on our main Web site, as well as add a short blogroll. We'll also show how to change a few more basic things.

We can add a picture and up to 1,200 characters about ourselves to the sidebar by editing our user profile. The user profile can be accessed from the initial window that appears after logging in to Blogger. (See Figure 8.10.)

There are many items in our profile that can be set. We are going to only set two, a photograph and the "About Me" section,

FIGURE 8.10 *Accessing the User Profile*

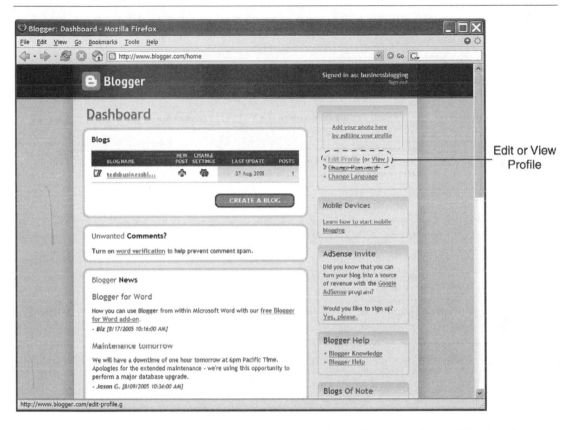

which will be automatically displayed in our sidebar. The other items are not displayed automatically. (See Figure 8.11.)

Note that we have the option to unset "Share my profile" if we want our profile information to remain private, and that the fields under "Identity"—Username, Email Address, and Display Name—are automatically set from data we provided when originally setting up our blog a few minutes ago.

In this case, Ted added a URL to a picture of himself from his company's Web site. If we didn't have a picture already on the Web or anywhere to put it, we could use Hello.com to publish pictures to any Blogger blog. Pictures are automatically transferred and

FIGURE 8.11 *Editing the User Profile*

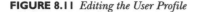

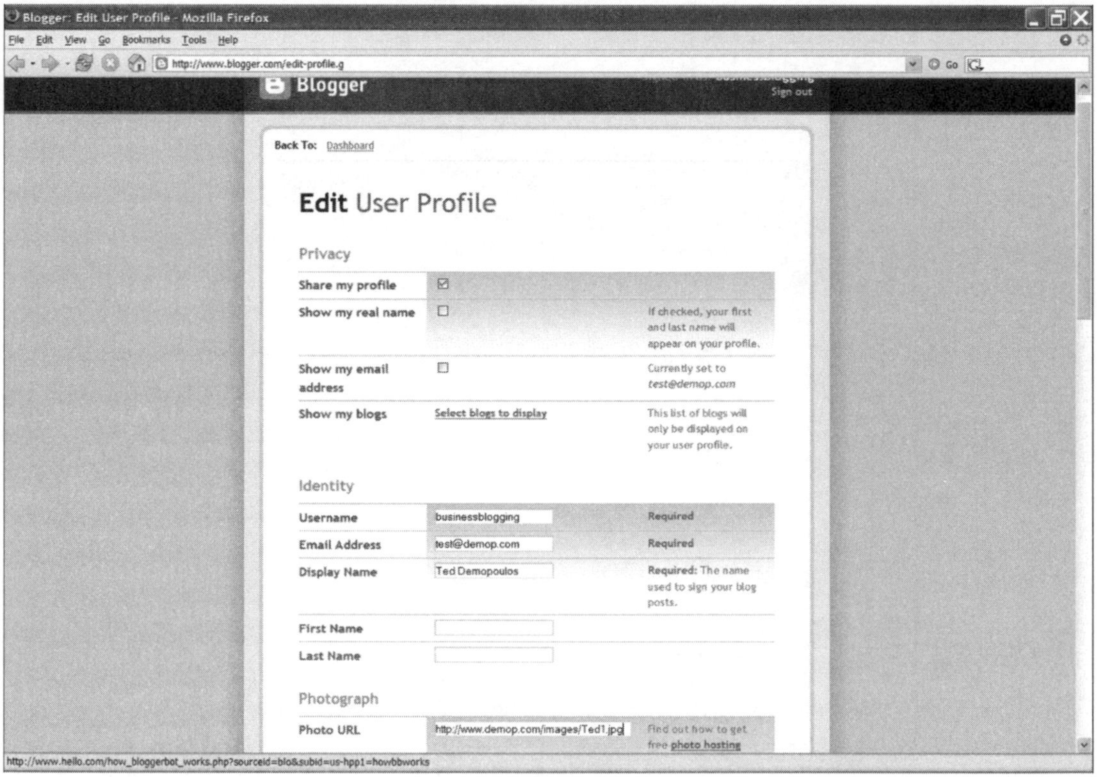

resized appropriately, and if you are using Blogger and blogspot hosting (the default), the pictures are also hosted for free.

We also scroll down in the "Edit User Profile" window and write a few words for the "About Me" Section. We can come back later and fill in additional fields in the profile if we'd like. Unless we make our profile private, people will be able to see it; for example, visitors to our blog as well as anyone on whose blog we leave a comment. Private profiles will still have their photo and "About Me" section displayed in the blog. We save the profile by clicking "Save Profile." (See Figure 8.12.)

Notice the changes to the blog. Both a picture and some text about Ted appear in the sidebar. The text is a somewhat silly

FIGURE 8.12 *The "About Me" Section of the User Profile*

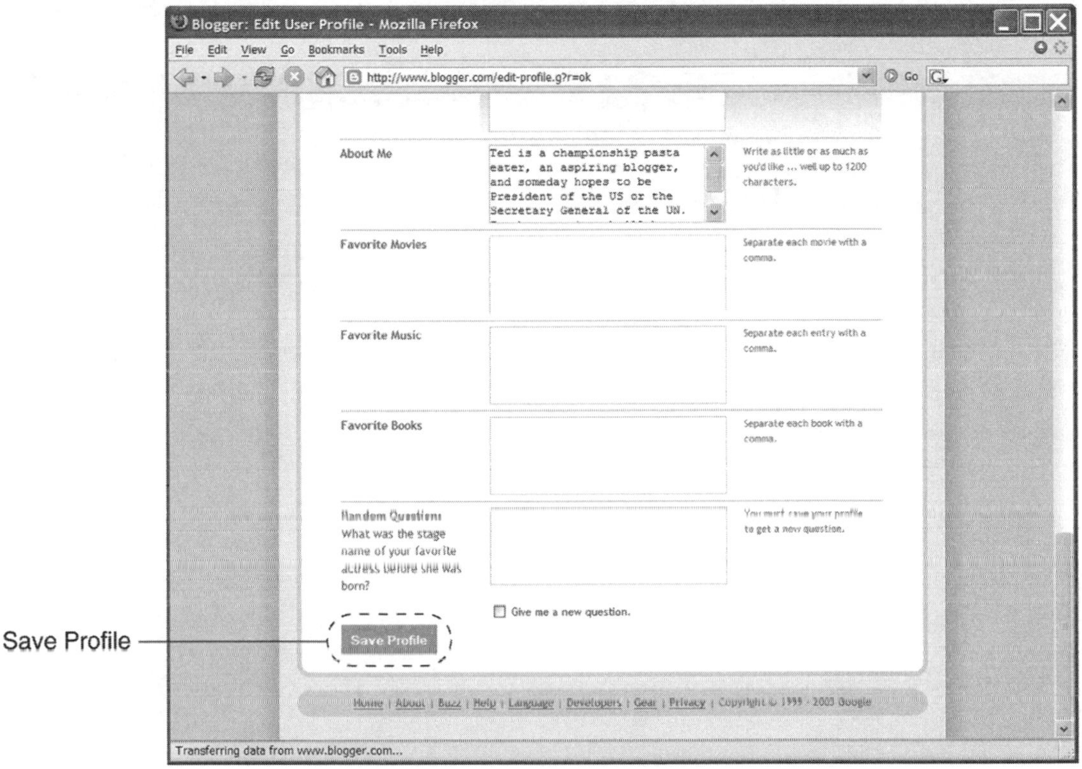

description of Ted, and if this were to be a serious business blog, we would recommend it be modified! (See Figure 8.13.)

Notice that slightly further down in the profile, you can see "LINKS" and presumably three links, one to Google News and two that say "Edit-Me." If we click on "Edit-Me," we actually get directions on how to edit the links.

In Blogger, editing the links requires editing the template, which is written in HTML. HTML is a very simple language and it is easy to make minor changes without understanding much about HTML. However, HTML is a programming language, and that scares many people. We are not attempting to teach you HTML; there are several excellent beginner tutorials available on

FIGURE 8.13 *Blog Displaying New Profile Information*

the Internet. Many, maybe even most, bloggers never touch HTML either. However, in Blogger it's required, and with most other blogging software, it's required for full flexibility.

We're just going to demonstrate that doing a few things in HTML is not hard at all. Also, Blogger's online help is superb and very task-oriented; it assumes you don't know HTML and probably don't want to learn it to do basic things. For those that want the full details of what can be done with Blogger's templates, you'll find the help superb as well.

Template Overview

Here is an overview of template formats. Most templates, including Blogger.com's, are written in HTML, although the code of other languages, such as JavaScript, may appear as well. HTML describes to a browser how to display a Web page, whether it's a part of a blog or anything else.

```
<html>
<head>
<!-- header information about this document, which is NOT dis-
played on the page -->
</head>

<body>

<!-- the HTML for display -->

    .

    .

    .

</body>
</html>
```

The code above creates a standard HTML file or "document," which describes a Web page, or in our case, a blog template. HTML files are standard text files, with "tags." Tags are text enclosed by the "<" and ">" characters. The entire contents of this document are enclosed by <html> and </html>. Within the <html> tags there are two parts, a "head" and a "body." Quite simply, the information in the head section is *not* displayed on the page. It can contain a title for the page, "meta" tags used by some search engines, defaults for fonts, font sizes, and colors, etc. The body contains information that will be displayed. Anything enclosed by "<!--" and "-->" is a comment, something added to enhance human readability, which is never displayed or interpreted. For example, <!-- the HTML for display -->, does nothing except add a comment to make the HTML document easier to read.

```
<html>
 <head>
<!-- head information about this document, which is NOT dis-
played on the page -->
</head>

<body>
    <div id="header">
    <!-- In "header," we have everything that appears at the top, like
    the title, description, etc. -->
    </div>

    <!-- Begin #content -->
    <div id="content">

        <!-- Begin #main -->
        <div id="main">

        <!--In "main," we have post and comment information -->

        </div>
        <!-- End #main -->

        <!-- Begin #sidebar -->
        <div id="sidebar">

        <!--"Sidebar" information goes here -->

        </div>
        <!-- End #sidebar -->
```

```
    </div>
    <!-- End #content -->

  </body>
  </html>
```

Above is the outline of a Blogger template. Most others are similar in concept if not actual format. We see there is more detail added in the "body" section than our generic HTML document outline shown previously.

Note that there are individual sections set apart by <div id= "somename"> and </div>. Although these section names can vary, we have a header and a content area. If we wanted to add or modify something at the top of our blog page, we would modify the header area of the template. The content area, which describes a blog's main content, is further broken down into a main area and sidebar area. The main area describes the format of the posts and contents, and the sidebar area describes the sidebar. If we wanted to add something to the sidebar, perhaps a picture, some text, a map, a calendar, or anything else, we would modify the sidebar area of the template.

We edit templates via the template editor (note that if you pick a new template, any previous customization needs to be re-done). (See Figure 8.14.)

The template editor is almost absurdly primitive. No search, no replace, limited undo functionality, and no ability to return to previously saved versions of the template. It is, however, very simple and straightforward to use. We strongly recommend cutting and pasting a copy of the template into a text editor and saving it into a file each time before editing just in case you want to revert to a previous template.

We have scrolled down in the template editor to the section that describes the links. Because the links are in the sidebar, it should be no surprise that we find them in the sidebar area of the template. To edit them, we simply modify the URL and the text that follows.

FIGURE 8.14 *The Blogger.com Template Editor*

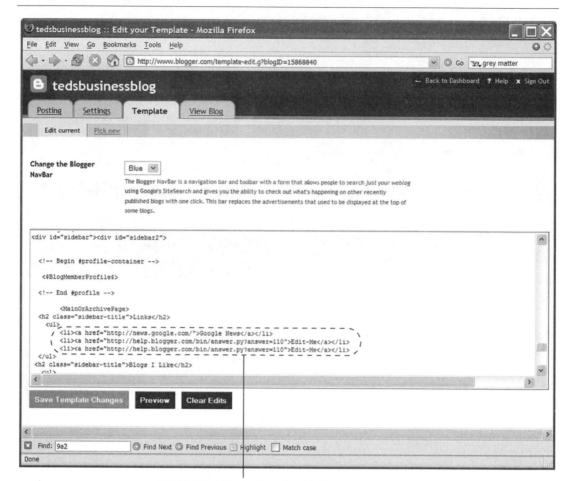

HTML That Describes the Links

For example, we modify:

```
<li><a href="http://news.google.com/">Google News</a></li>
```

to:

```
<li><a href="http://www.demop.com/">Demopoulos Associates </a></li>
```

to change the link to say "Demopoulos Associates" and point to http://www.demop.com.

We can have as many links as we want, but we leave the three and modify them to link to various parts of Ted's company's Web site with appropriate text. We use the "Preview" button to make sure everything looks OK (screen shot not shown), before we hit the "Save Template Changes" button. (See Figure 8.15.)

FIGURE 8.15 *Modifying "Links" in the Template Editor*

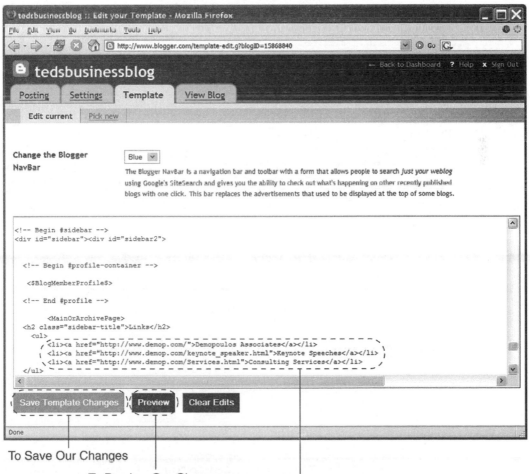

To Save Our Changes

To Preview Our Changes

Modified HTML with Our Desired Links

Although we have saved our changes, we still need to republish before the changes take effect (i.e., become visible on the blog). Modifying the template always requires saving changes and republishing. (See Figure 8.16.)

Notice the links have changed. It is best to "test" each link by clicking on it to make sure it works. (See Figure 8.17.)

We are now going to add a blogroll. We could use an add-on like BlogRolls, which would allow us to make changes to our blogroll without modifying HTML, although it would still require initially modifying the HTML to implement BlogRolls' functionality. Instead we are going to do the simplest thing possible, at least from

FIGURE 8.16 *Template Editor after Saving Edits*

Republish to Make Our Changes Visible

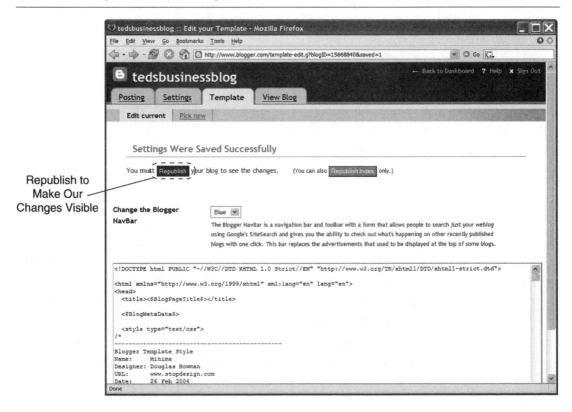

FIGURE 8.17 *Viewing the Blog with the Edited Template*

Ted's perspective: modify the HTML template file using the copy and paste technique. (See Figure 8.18.)

A blogroll is simply a list of links. We already have a list of links, so we'll just copy, paste, and modify it. We see the highlighted HTML code in the template above that we are going to copy. We paste another copy right below the original so that our blogroll comes right after our links section in the sidebar, but we could put it anywhere we want. We modify the copied HTML, just like before, to point to some blogs we like. We also change the new title from "LINKS" to "Blogs I Like." We can have as many blogs in our blogroll as we want, but we start with only three. Remem-

FIGURE 8.18 *Copying and Pasting in the Template*

ber to preview to make sure it looks fine, then save and republish. (See Figure 8.19.)

We test the links to make sure they work fine—a typo could easily have crept in that would affect the functionality of the links. Notice our first post has five comments already, in just about 20 minutes. Something is very fishy. We click on the word "COMMENTS" to see them. (See Figure 8.20.)

Five spam comments on a brand new blog in less than five minutes!! Unfortunately, this probably isn't some kind of record, although it's the worst that we've seen. Comment and other types of spam keep getting worse. We can (and will) delete these com-

FIGURE 8.19 *Blog with Blogroll Added*

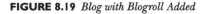

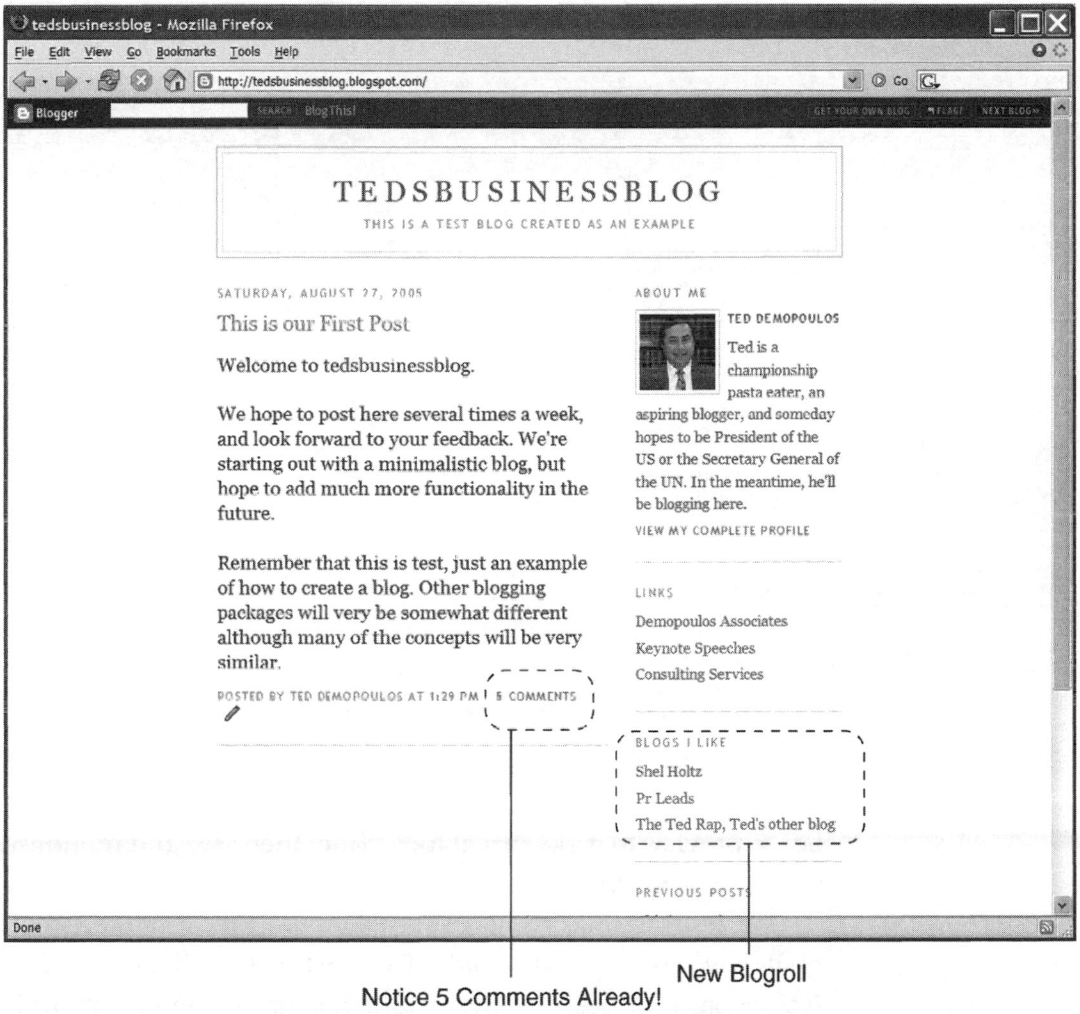

Notice 5 Comments Already!   New Blogroll

ments, but for now let's see how we can prevent our blog from getting more of them.

By default, Blogger allows only registered users to leave comments. The other choices are to allow comments from anyone or
only members of your blog. The "Only Registered Users" option
only allows users with a Blogger login account to leave messages.

FIGURE 8.20 *Spam Comments*

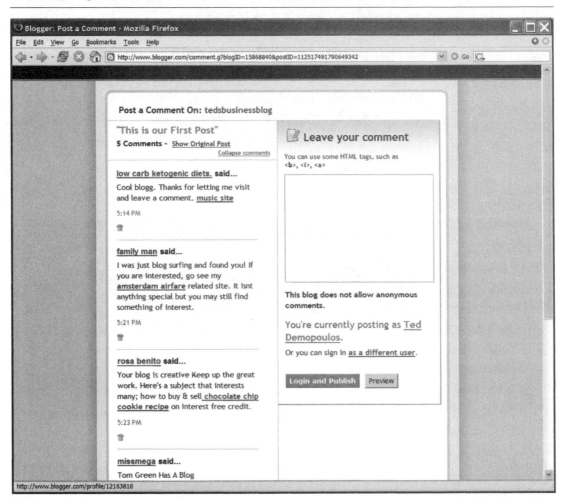

This cuts down on spam comments because many automated software robots cannot log in, but it obviously doesn't eliminate them all. It also tends to reduce the amount of legitimate comments because not everyone who wants to comment will be motivated enough to get a Blogger account if they don't have one. The "Only Members of This Blog" option means only users who are allowed to make new posts can leave comments. We only have one registered user, Ted, but could allow several users and hence have a multiauthor blog. Eventually, we'll change this to the "Anyone" option, but we'll leave it as is now.

Where it asks the question "Show word verification for comments?" we chose "Yes," which will turn on CAPTCHA functionality for making comments. CAPTCHA is an acronym for completely automated public Turing test to tell computers and humans apart, and uses a distorted graphic of a word to differentiate between a computer (e.g., an automated software robot) and a human user. (See Figure 8.21.)

FIGURE 8.21 *Comment Settings*

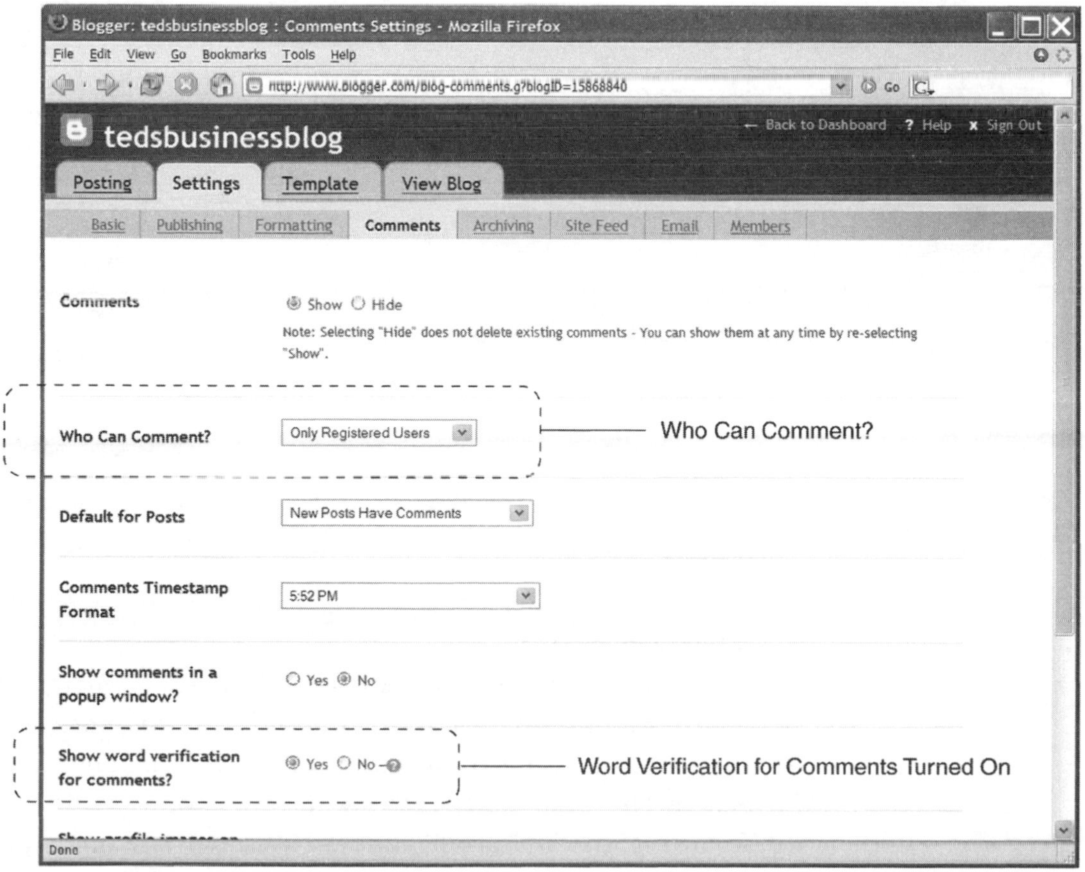

Notice now that in order to leave a comment it is necessary to type in the text from the CAPTCHA, the distorted image. This stops almost 100 percent of spam comments because automated software robots cannot (at least as of yet) read CAPTCHAs. (See Figure 8.22.)

FIGURE 8.22 *CAPTCHA Protection for Spam Comment Prevention*

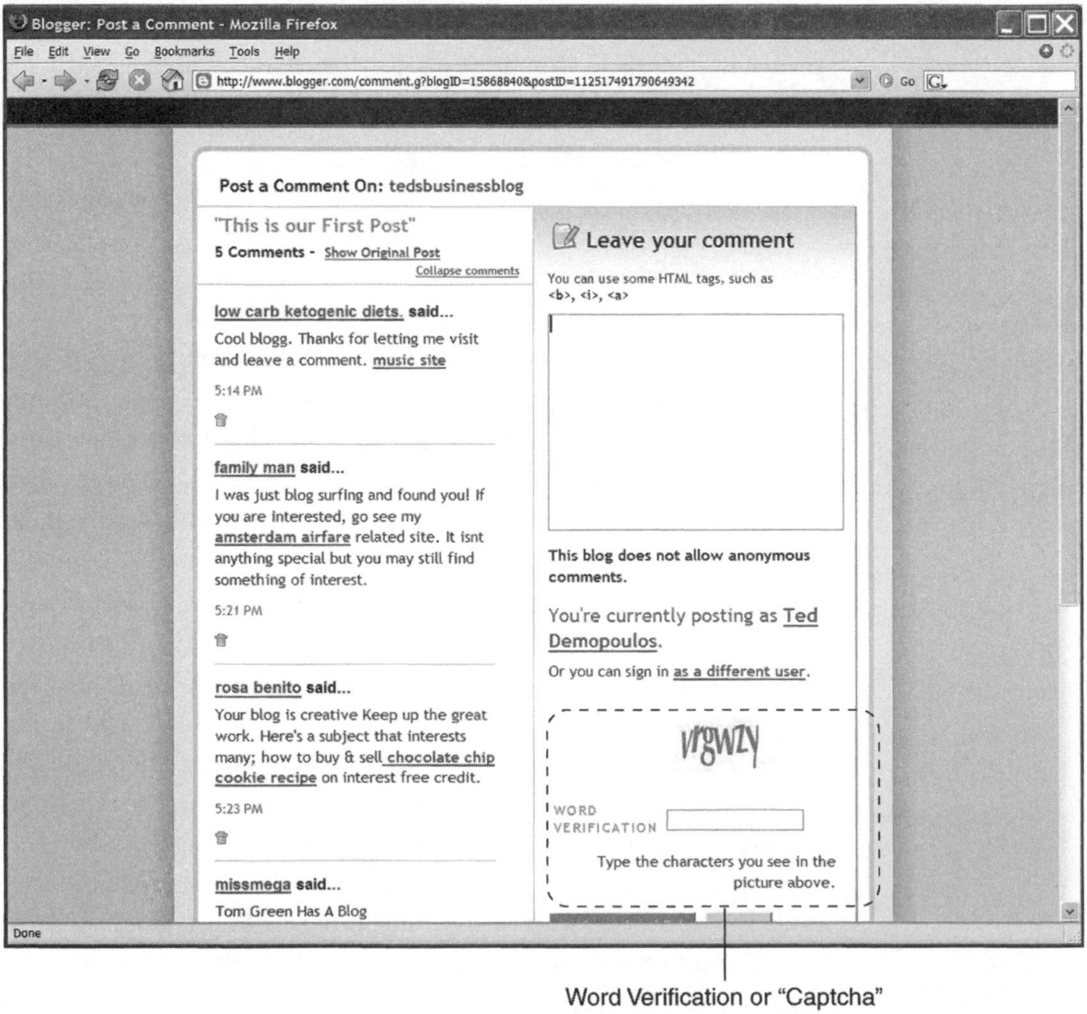

Word Verification or "Captcha"

ADDITIONAL MODIFICATIONS AND ADD-ONS

There are many add-ons and modifications we can make. Very often a blog's template and functionality will evolve over time. We'll look at a few common things that can be added or changed, but basically the sky is the limit.

A lot of add-on functionality requires adding small sections of code to the template. Although not difficult, it can require some trial and error. Today, some executives still have their secretaries print out e-mails to which they then dictate responses. Clearly not everyone is going to be comfortable manually editing templates, even among those that are tech savvy.

Google AdSense

A lot of blogs carry advertising (we discussed pros and cons of having advertising on your blog in Chapter 6). Google AdSense is one of the most popular. Google AdSense places context-sensitive advertisements on your blog, or any Web page. There is very little control over what advertisements are displayed, although you can control where on the screen they appear. You can exclude specific ads by URL, so you can exclude competitors' advertisements if you like, as well as any advertisements you might find objectionable. Google determines which advertisements to place on your page by context—by looking at what else is on that page. Sometimes the choices might seem bizarre. A comment about the Vatican and technology on Ted's blog once caused a two-week barrage of Pope advertisements, Christian singles advertisements, Catholic literature advertisements, etc., that were essentially impossible to stop without disabling AdSense itself. Because Ted doesn't discuss religion on his blog, the advertisements were very out of place and several readers commented on that! (See Figure 8.23.)

FIGURE 8.23 *Google AdSense Advertisements on The Ted Rap*

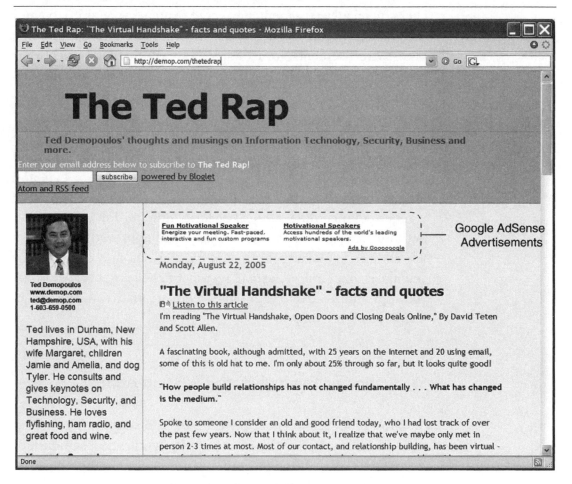

Note the two Google AdSense advertisements about one-third of the way down for "Fun Motivational Speaker" and "Motivational Speakers."

We've just been describing Google AdSense for Content. There is also Google AdSense for Search, which places a small Google search box on your Web site. When visitors search using your Google search box, they are returned organic search results as well as advertisements targeting the keywords on which they searched.

Your AdSense account is credited money every time someone clicks on an advertisement, anywhere from a few pennies to a few dollars. Visitors do not need to buy anything, unlike with some other advertisements, for example those of the Amazon.com Associates program. Google AdWords is the other side of Google's advertisement equation. With AdWords, people pay to have traffic delivered to them via clicks on AdSense advertisements.

Setting up AdSense is easy, although it requires the addition of some code to your template. First, you need to sign up for an AdSense account and be approved. This takes a day or two, and almost everyone is approved. Quite a bit of personal information is required, including a Social Security number for U.S. citizens, because AdSense income is taxable. Once approved, there are a few choices to make regarding ad type, layout, and colors. Once you make your choices, a small section of code is generated which you copy and paste into your blog's template, then save and republish. (See Figure 8.24.)

Syndication or Feeds, Including RSS and Atom

Most blogging software provides built-in support for syndication. Currently, RSS is the most popular syndication standard or format for feeds, although Atom is a popular yet competing standard. Surprisingly, Blogger only supports Atom today.

Unfortunately, we have three versions of RSS in common use, 0.91, 1.0, and 2.0, and two versions of the competing Atom specification. Fortunately, many applications that handle RSS can read any version including Atom so this isn't as big a problem as it might appear at first. Many Web sites also make multiple versions of RSS available, typically 1.0 and 2.0, as well as Atom. Someday Atom and RSS may merge, but the two camps are quite contentious today.

Some software, for example Windows Vista and Internet Explorer, will support all these different syndication formats: RSS

FIGURE 8.24 *Some Google AdSense Formats*

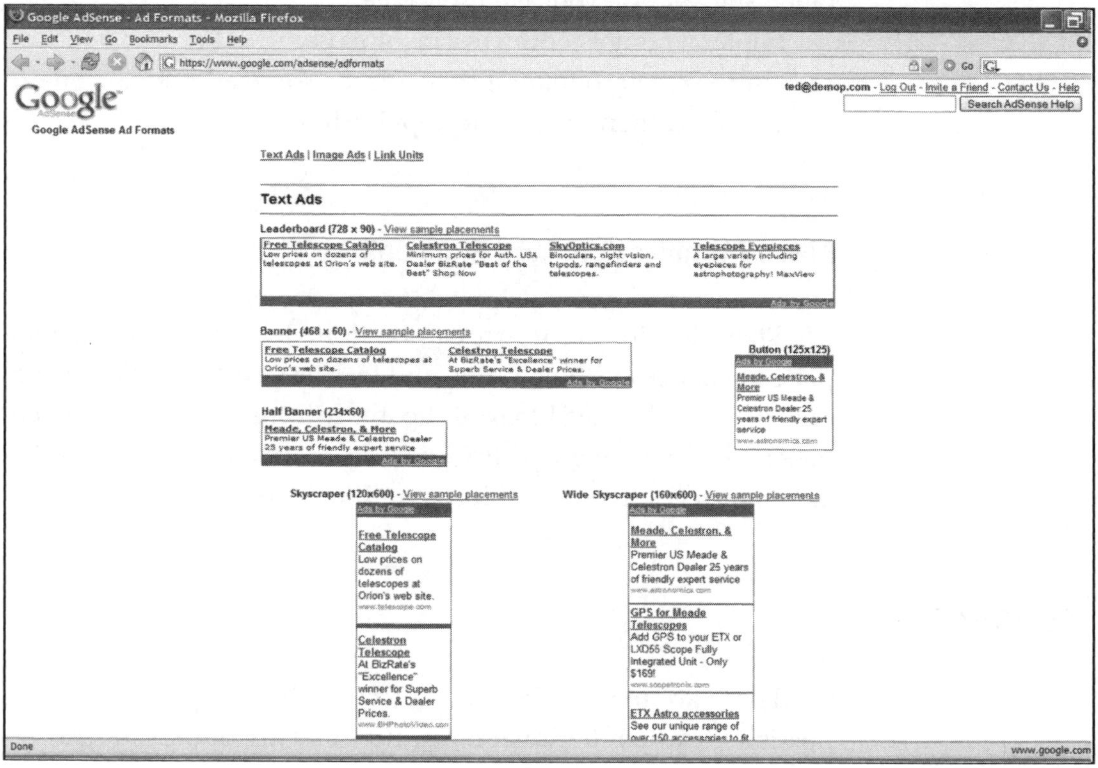

0.9x, RSS 1.0, RSS 2.0, Atom 0.3, and Atom 1.0. Many feedreaders can read multiple formats/versions as well, but support for all versions of RSS and Atom is far from universal.

FeedBurner is an interesting free service that avoids Atom and RSS version and format compatibility issues. FeedBurner's SmartFeed™ server takes an Atom or RSS feed in any version and makes it available to feedreaders in whatever format they support, any version of RSS or Atom. FeedBurner also provides statistics on feed circulation, which feedreaders people are using to read your feed, and which feed items subscribers most often "click through" to go to your site. There are a number of additional Feed-Burner services available, including adding Google AdSense ads to your feed, and a pro statistics package which delivers more detailed statistics on your feed for a fee.

Implementing FeedBurner involves going to FeedBurner.com, creating a free account and then adding some additional code to the template, then saving and republishing.

More Modifications and Add-ons

There is a lot more that can be done by modifying the template to change the blog's look and feel, as well as additional add-ons such as enhanced blogroll capability from BlogRolls .com, enhanced commenting and trackbacks from Haloscan.com, and e-mail interfaces from FeedBlitz.com, Bloglet.com and others.

SUMMARY

There are many different choices for blogging software. It is possible to switch between blogging software, but it can be difficult, so it's worth spending some time to choose a solution that has the functionality your organization requires.

It is easy to create a blog. However, setting up blogging software and customizing a blog are not. Many organizations and professionals will no doubt get an IT professional, graphic designer, or blogging consultant to set up their blogging software, and then create and tweak their blog. However, knowing how to make some basic modifications can be very useful. Once a blog is set up, it's time to start posting and promoting it.

Unfortunately, you need to do more than just create a blog and add posts to attract an audience. You need to write interesting and useful posts, and somehow let the world know. We discuss publicizing your blog in the following chapters.

9

PROMOTING YOUR BLOG

You've launched your blog. Congratulations, and welcome to the blogosphere! Now you have to let the world know it's there and give people a reason to want to read it. After all, the blogosphere is not a *Field of Dreams;* they won't come just because you built it. Your customers need to know you have a blog, where it is, and why they should add it to the already-time-consuming volume of content they read.

A host of promotion techniques can be sorted into three basic categories:

1. Self-promotion
2. Listings
3. Social networking

SELF-PROMOTION

The most effective ways to create awareness of your blog are in your control. You don't need to subscribe to any services or hope somebody else will point to you.

Tell Everybody

You've gone to the trouble of creating a blog and you know what you want it to accomplish for your organization. Don't be ashamed of it. Don't be shy. Put the word out. Use every opportunity to tout the blog's existence and the benefits it offers its target audience.

Start with your own Web site home page. Far too many organizations have launched blogs and buried them within their sites, making them all but impossible to find. A casual visitor to the site would never know a blog is available because there is no link to it on the home page. Access to your blog should be clearly marked on your home page, at the very least as a link on your top-level navigation bar.

You can go well beyond this permanent home page link to the blog in the days immediately following the launch. Most businesses use the most visible home page real estate for current news and promotions. It's an ideal location for an announcement about your new corporate blog.

In addition to linking to your blog from the home page, you should also make sure the blog is accessible from the pages with content relating to the blog. For example, let's say you work for an airline. You have five blogs. A page titled "Our Blogs" lists all of the blogs written by employees. But a link to each blog can also be found on related pages:

- Recruiting blog—linked from the recruiting page
- Customer service blog—linked from any page customers may visit when looking for help

- Travel tips blog—linked from reservation pages along with any pages listing vacation packages and special deals
- Frequent flyer blog—linked from the frequent flyer page
- CEO blog—linked from the top-level page

This is one of the techniques organizations most often fail to recognize. Despite the fact that Matt Brown, Macromedia's community manager for its Dreamweaver Web development software, maintains his own blog, you can't find it from the Dreamweaver product page on the Macromedia Web site.

In addition to links on your Web site, a press release can also raise awareness and drive traffic to your blog. Take advantage of any press release distribution services you already have, such as an account with PR Newswire or Business Wire. Be sure to target the release to publications and other media to which your target audience pays attention. A pharmaceutical company with a blog aimed at doctors wouldn't attract the right kind of attention by sending a press release to editors of weekly community newspapers; medical trade publications would be ideal.

The World Wide Web is home to a number of online press release distribution services. A useful list of sites that host or distribute press releases is at http://www.softwaremarketingresource.com/pressreleases.html. Many of these resources are free; many others are remarkably inexpensive.

Write Great Content

You only need a few readers to create awareness of your blog, assuming the content you create is compelling enough for your few readers to link to your blog on *their* blogs. Staying on point is one of the most important ways you can get your readers to want to link to your copy.

Look, for instance, at General Motors' FastLane blog. In its strategic planning for the blog, General Motors' communicators determined the blog would remain focused strictly on cars. Since launching the blog, GM has come under routine pressure to discuss current issues, such as financial performance and labor problems. FastLane has, despite this pressure, remained true to its target audience of car enthusiasts. If GM Vice Chairman Bob Lutz, Fast-Lane's principal blogger, began using FastLane to address topics car enthusiasts don't care about, those dedicated readers would start drifting away. The more that car enthusiasts read the site, the more those with their own blogs are likely to link to the GM blog, raising its visibility both among readers of *their* blogs and on search engines. (We'll look specifically at optimizing your blogs for search engines in Chapter 10.)

As you can see from the screen capture in Figure 9.1, plenty of people link to the GM blog. In this case, the buzz was started when Lutz was interviewed for the first time on the blog's associated podcast.

Lutz and his team understand that car enthusiasts want to read about cars. And not just the typical corporate communications marketers and PR departments release, but original material they can't get anywhere else, written in an authentic voice and offering the personal insights of the senior-most executive responsible for vehicles.

It's also important that you blog frequently. Maintaining interest in your blog won't be easy if you're posting only two or three times a month. Post at least weekly, and, ideally, a few times a week.

Enhance Subscription Possibilities

Blogging utilities, as we have noted earlier, automatically generate feeds using standards like RSS and Atom. Corporate blogs that don't enable feeds are roundly criticized in the blogosphere, and there is no earthly reason to subject your organization to the same criticism. Some IT departments worry about the bandwidth

FIGURE 9.1 *Recent Citations from Top-Ranked Blogs*

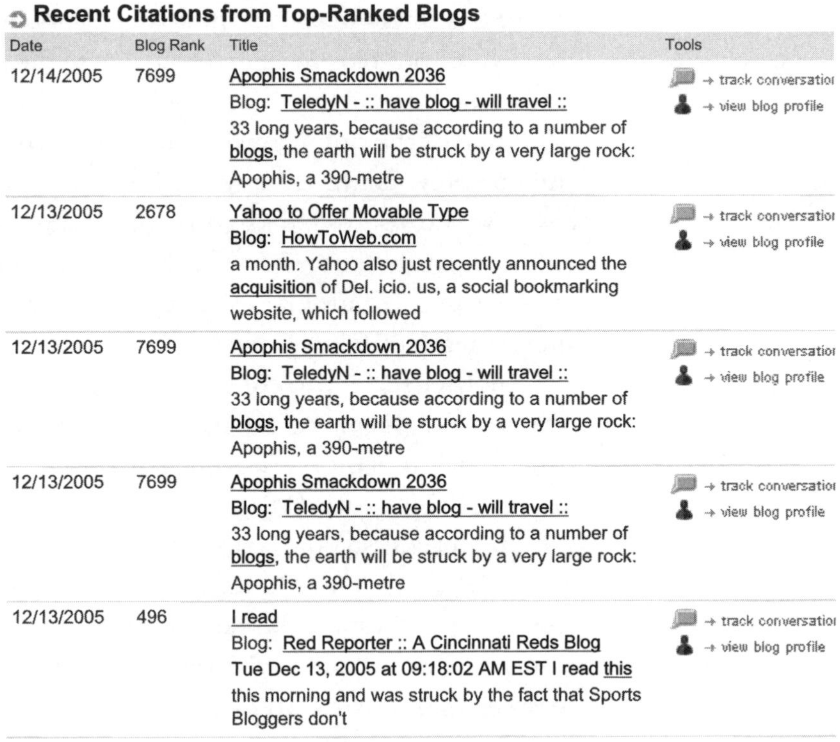

↻ Recent Citations from Top-Ranked Blogs

Date	Blog Rank	Title	Tools
12/14/2005	7699	**Apophis Smackdown 2036** Blog: <u>TeledyN - :: have blog - will travel ::</u> 33 long years, because according to a number of <u>blogs</u>, the earth will be struck by a very large rock: Apophis, a 390-metre	→ track conversation → view blog profile
12/13/2005	2678	**Yahoo to Offer Movable Type** Blog: <u>HowToWeb.com</u> a month. Yahoo also just recently announced the <u>acquisition</u> of Del. icio. us, a social bookmarking website, which followed	→ track conversation → view blog profile
12/13/2005	7699	**Apophis Smackdown 2036** Blog: <u>TeledyN - :: have blog - will travel ::</u> 33 long years, because according to a number of <u>blogs</u>, the earth will be struck by a very large rock: Apophis, a 390-metre	→ track conversation → view blog profile
12/13/2005	7699	**Apophis Smackdown 2036** Blog: <u>TeledyN - :: have blog - will travel ::</u> 33 long years, because according to a number of <u>blogs</u>, the earth will be struck by a very large rock: Apophis, a 390-metre	→ track conversation → view blog profile
12/13/2005	496	**I read** Blog: <u>Red Reporter :: A Cincinnati Reds Blog</u> Tue Dec 13, 2005 at 09:18:02 AM EST I read <u>this</u> this morning and was struck by the fact that Sports Bloggers don't	→ track conversation → view blog profile

demands their servers would face if the blog became enormously popular. Of course, if the feed is that popular, that means it's succeeding and an increase in bandwidth to accommodate the demand should be easy to justify. (As an alternative, you can take advantage of services like Nooked.com that host Web feeds for you.)

But don't stop when you've created a link to your Web feed. You can enhance the value of your feed by tapping into some of the feed-related services available on the Web.

For example, you can add the means for subscribers to choose Feedburner.com for their subscription. When visitors click the Feedburner.com link, they get a page that displays your most recent posts along with instructions for subscribing. Further, when you go through Feedburner.com, you can tap into the statistics the service makes available. (We'll talk more about using Feedburner.com for measurement purposes when we talk about measuring the effectiveness of your blog in Chapter 11. These measurement capabilities lead some bloggers to offer *only* Feedburner.com subscriptions.)

Some of the online feedreaders (also called RSS newsreaders) such as NewsGator, Bloglines, MyMSN, and MyYahoo make it easy for you to post links so readers who already use these services can easily subscribe. Clicking the link takes you to the newsreader site and automatically subscribes your blog to the list of subscribed feeds.

Another service to consider accommodates the many readers who are not yet using feedreaders. This service enables e-mail subscriptions. Live Message Alerts is a free service of the Microsoft Network (MSN). By completing a form at http://signup.alerts.msn.com, you'll get the code to add to your page that will create a link to an e-mail subscription tool. Visitors to your site who want to be notified via e-mail about your most recent posts simply click the link and complete the form. Other services mentioned earlier that can also enable e-mail subscriptions include FeedBlitz.com and BotABlog.com.

Talk Up the Blog

You might be surprised at the number of places you can refer to your blog in order to heighten awareness. Here's a short list of opportunities you should not ignore:

- *Business cards.* Include the link on your business cards along with your Web site URL.
- *E-mail signatures.* Most e-mail software supports e-mail signatures, which appear as a block of text automatically appended to the bottom of each e-mail message. It is very common to

include the sender's name, e-mail address and other contact details, company Web site, etc. Many bloggers also include their blog information. How you include your blog information is something worth considering. Shel simply has a line that says "Blog: http://blog.holtz.com." Ted currently has "Visit The Ted Rap Blog." in his signature, where The Ted Rap Blog is a hyperlink. Previously, Ted simply had "Visit The Ted Rap," which people tended to ignore because it was confusing. "What is The Ted Rap?" was a common question. Both Ted and Shel's current choices are very clear and unambiguous, to those who know what a blog is. Most people do not know what a blog is. A description of the blog could be used in the signature; for example, "Visit The Ted Rap, Ted's thoughts on IT, security, business, and more." A description might be particularly useful and appropriate when e-mailing people less likely to be familiar with blogs.

- *Presentations.* The final slide on any PowerPoint presentation (or whatever presentation software you use) almost always includes contact information, such as a phone number and e-mail address. Add the URL for your blog to this slide.
- *Trade show materials.* Companies that rent out booths at trade shows spend a small fortune printing materials for attendees to take home in the hopes that the collection of takeaways helps the attendees remember the company after they get back to the office. In addition to brochures and fact sheets, companies give away imprinted pens, retractable Ethernet cables, magnets, mugs, mouse pads, squeeze balls, and an endless supply of other promotional materials onto which you can add the blog's URL.
- *Press releases.* Add the link to your blog in the boilerplate of your press release template.
- *Advertising.* Ongoing online and offline company advertising campaigns can mention blogs. For example, a billboard or other print advertisement could include a blog name and

URL. Specific advertising campaigns can be initiated as well. Recently, some blogs have been using banner ads on Web sites and some blogs have been advertising using Google Ad-Words (the flip side of Google AdSense). The advertising of blogs is a relatively new phenomenon.

Enhance Your Blog's Searchability

You can take a number of steps to ensure your blog is found when readers conduct searches for content that matches yours. These include the following:

- Give your blog a name that references its theme. For example, a blog about a product should include the product name. One addressing an issue should have a name that includes the issue.
- Assign each post to a category. Several of the blog search engines, such as Technorati, view categories as "tags," which can be searched independently of the rest of the words in the post.
- Tag posts. Tagging allows you to identify key words that readers may use when searching for information on the subject of the post.

Include a Blogroll

We've already discussed blogrolls, and in the next chapter, we'll talk about getting your blog into other bloggers' blogrolls. But you can get considerable mileage when promoting your blog by setting up your own blogroll of other blogs.

How can linking to other blogs drive traffic to your own? Most of the blog search engines spider blogrolls; as a result, it's easy for a blogger to find out who's linking to them. To your blogroll, you should add the blogs that already have attracted the audience you're after. The bloggers will find their blogs in your blogroll and will undoubtedly visit your blog to find out who you are. If they like what they see, they could write about you or reciprocate by adding your blog to *their* blogrolls.

Blogrolls, by the way, take a lot of work, but a free service called Blogrolling.com simplifies the process of maintaining these important tools.

Encourage Return Traffic to Your Blog

Hopefully a lot of people will visit your blog. Certainly most blogs have far more visitors than regular readers. Getting visitors to return is extremely important to establishing a well-read blog.

Having an inviting and easy-to-read blog is an important step. Garish colors, strange fonts, and difficult-to-decipher text/background color combinations need to be avoided. If the visual appearance of your blog gives the reader a headache or trying to read it gives visitors eyestrain, don't expect them to return. It's also critical, as we keep emphasizing, to have good content.

It is very common for someone to find a Web site or blog they like and plan to return to later, but despite best intentions never do. In order to get visitors to become regular readers you should make getting back to your site easy. Allow your visitors options—you can't assume anything. They might prefer to type your blog's URL into their browser every time. Provide a URL, or alternate URL, that is easy to remember and enter. They might want to receive your posts via e-mail, even though you think they should subscribe via RSS. Even if you think your visitors are technology averse, you should still provide easy ways to subscribe to your RSS feed.

Give your blog an easy-to-remember URL. One evening over dinner, one of Ted's clients said he liked reading Ted's blog, but always forgot the URL or typed it in wrong. He admitted to occasionally absentmindedly typing in http://www.TheTedRap .com instead of http://www.demop.com/TheTedRap. Ted's first thought was to tell his client to join the modern world and use a feedreader, or at the very least bookmark The Ted Rap in his browser. Instead, a virtual lightbulb went off in Ted's head and he said, "I'll try to fix that for you." Later that night Ted had ob tained the URL http://www.TheTedRap.com and set it up to automatically redirect to his blog. Investment? Maybe ten minutes online and less than $20 a year. The Ted Rap saw an immediate jump in traffic! Apparently, others also sometimes typed in http:/ /www.TheTedRap .com when trying to get to Ted's blog.

If your blog's URL is difficult to remember, you might consider a similar approach. Sure, you could move your blog, but that will probably result in some readers not following along. If your blog's URL is something simple like http://blog.holtz.com or http://www.nevon.net, you are fine, but if your blog's name is more similar to http://www.DemopoulosAssociatesAndSon.com/ americasdivision/east/qwerty/aggamemnon/blog.html, you may want to consider some type of shortcut such as a simple domain name like http://www.aggiesblog.com that will redirect people to your blog.

Implement an e-mail interface. One option that many people prefer is subscribing to your blog using their e-mail address and then having future blog posts mailed to them automatically. Some bloggers almost recoil with horror at this thought, feeling that readers are supposed to either visit the blog directly from their browser or consume its contents via its RSS or Atom feed using a feedreader. What you want people to do and what they want to do are often quite different. You might, like many bloggers, think e-mail is inappropriate for blog posts, but a surprising number of people prefer it!

It's easy to add e-mail subscription functionality to your blog. There are several free services available including FeedBlitz.com and BotABlog.com, or you or someone in your IT department can develop your own. Ted uses FeedBlitz.com. With this service, you can choose whether to have entire posts or partial posts e-mailed, and examine e-mail addresses to see who signed up.

Make it easy to subscribe using popular feedreaders. RSS/ Atom penetration is estimated to be between a single-digit percentage to a very low double-digit percentage depending on the study, but it is expected to grow rapidly because RSS functionality is built in to Microsoft Windows Vista and Internet Explorer 7.0.

Some popular feedreaders include My Yahoo!, Bloglines, NewsGator, My MSN, and Pluck. Offering "one click" functionality for adding your blog to visitors' feedreaders can only increase readership. Easy is good, and this will allow visitors who haven't yet added your blog to their feedreaders to become regular readers. Notice the icons in the sidebar in Figure 9.2.

FIGURE 9.2 *"One Click" Functionality for Adding The Ted Rap to Popular Feedreaders*

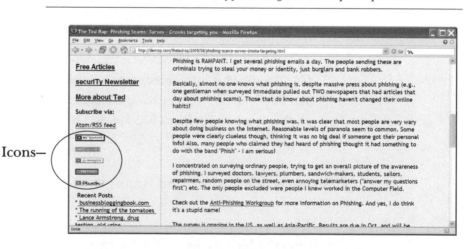

Icons—

Here is some example HTML code from The Ted Rap's sidebar. To make this code work for your blog you need to replace Ted's feed URL with yours, and add the HTML code in your template.

```
<p><a href="http://add.my.yahoo.com/content?url=http://feeds
.feedburner.com/TheTedRap">
<img src="http://us.i1.yimg.com/us.yimg.com/i/us/my/addtomyyahoo4
.gif" alt="Add to My Yahoo!"></a></p>

<p><a href="http://www.bloglines.com/sub/http://feeds.feedburner
.com/TheTedRap">
<img src= "http://www.bloglines.com/images/sub_modern5.gif" border
="0" alt="Subscribe with Bloglines" /></a></p>

<p> <a>href="http://www.newsgator.com/ngs/subscriber/subext.aspx
?url=http://feeds.feedburner.com/TheTedRap"> <img runat=
"server" src="http://www.newsgator.com/images/ngsub1.gif" alt=
"Subscribe in NewsGator Online" border="0"></a></p>

<p><a href="http://my.msn.com/addtomymsn.armx?id=rss&ut=http://
feeds.feedburner.com/TheTedRap">
<img src="http://sc.msn.com/44/G,UCH{ZBSS3{OS{SE469LG.gif">
</a></p>

<p><a href="http://client.pluck.com/pluckit/prompt.aspx?GCID=
C12286x053&a=http://feeds.feedburner.com/TheTedRap&t=The
Ted Rap"> <img src="http://client.pluck.com/pluckit/pluckit.png"
alt="Subscribe with Pluck RSS reader" border="0"/></a></p>
```

Give Away Research and Reports

A lot of organizations have created buzz and attracted attention by using the blog as the source for interesting and useful material your target audience will want to download. White papers and research reports—usually produced in the Adobe Acrobat PDF (portable document file) format—are incredibly popular among members of a target audience.

For example, a Web design firm conducted a simple set of usability tests to determine how well Web users understood the various elements of a blog. (Not well, as it turned out.) It produced the results in a detailed report and promoted the report on its blog. For readers who were already inclined to care about Web design, the report was right up their alley. It was downloaded extensively.

LISTINGS

Syndication

There are several online resources where you can list your feed, including Feedster, http://www.feedster.com, and Syndic8, http://www.syndic8.com. These services allow you to submit the URL of your feeds so others searching for feeds can find it.

Manual Listings

In some blogging communities, dedicated members maintain lists of bloggers. In the public relations community, Constantin Basturea maintains the best list of PR bloggers. Basturea uses Bloglines, http://www.bloglines.com/public/prblogs, to maintain a list of all the PR bloggers he knows about. Of course, one of the best ways for a PR blogger to get added to the list is to point Constantin to his blog.

SOCIAL NETWORKING

Participate in Blogging Communities

Once you're a blogger, you should act like one. Bloggers talk to one another as part of a blogging community, which can be either formal or informal. Formal discussions occur in message boards or on wikis dedicated to the community; informal communities can form in e-mail lists.

Because it is the cross-linkages between blogs that help build visibility and awareness, you can benefit greatly by building strong relationships with the other bloggers in your marketplace. Once they get to know you, they'll be more inclined to keep your blog on their must-read list of feeds and link to your blog whenever you write something that resonates with them.

If you're an executive blogger—someone of the stature of GM's Bob Lutz or Sun Microsystems' Jonathan Schwartz—you may not need the "link love" that comes from peers in the community. The very fact that you're a senior executive of a big company who is blogging could well generate all the publicity you need. For anybody else, though, it bodes well if you behave in a manner consistent with the conversational nature of the blogosphere. Remember, these are not isolated Web sites, but rather elements of a living, evolving entity whose life force is dialogue.

The relatively small set of some 400 public relations–focused blogs offers some insight into an informally organized community. Most PR bloggers read several—if not dozens—of the other PR blogs. They include each other on their blogrolls, link to each other's posts, and comment on each other's observations. Many collect e-mail addresses and notify the community at large when something interesting or important comes up.

In 2004, a number of the PR bloggers came together to produce Global PR Blog Week 1.0, a weeklong online event in which the various participants posted items consistent with the day's theme. Global PR Blog Week took place in September 2005, with more than 50 members of the community contributing posts. Each of those authors was now exposed to a new audience, attracting new readers to their blogs. This kind of self-organizing effort benefits all participants, but you have to *participate* in order to take advantage of these unique opportunities.

Comment On Other Blogs

Commenting on posts to blogs similar to your own is one of the fastest ways to get known among your target audience. When you submit a comment, most systems let you enter the URL of your blog, so anybody who reads what you had to say also can click a link and visit your blog.

Comments, according to many, are required as a core element of a blog. Not everyone agrees. Even Dave Winer, who developed the earliest blogging utilities, thinks comments are optional. If you want to comment on what he wrote, Winer suggested in an interview with the *Online Journalism Review,* you should do it on your own blog and link to his.

While Winer's argument has merit, comments are nonetheless viewed as integral to blogging.

As you read other blogs—particularly those that address the same issues and audience as your own blog—comment whenever you believe you have something salient to add to the conversation. Because you represent a business, your comments should *never* reflect anything other than your company's values. Profanity, attacks, poor taste, and other characteristics won't serve your company's reputation well. Instead, your posts should offer insights and explanations, serving generally as a public service to the community of readers. If your comments strike a chord, readers will find their way to your blog.

Ted left the following comment on Bruce Schneier's popular Schneier on Security blog in response to a post titled "Lance Armstrong Accused of Doping."

> This has implications potentially beyond sports—employees are often drug tested as well.
>
> I always refuse on principle to give urine samples, and AM occasionally asked by clients. My principles are for sale however! On several occasions I have offered to "sell my urine" for US$5,000 per vial.
>
> Hey, it's mine! No takers so far. BTW, my urine should test "clean," except for an abundance of caffeine.

It was not a flip comment: Ted is a consultant, and reporting to a lab takes time and incurs client charges. It is also authentic, being entirely in character. This comment resulted in significant return traffic.

Most blogs' comment systems allow you to enter your URL or the pathname to your blog, or use a free login system such as TypeKey. These all perform the same function—allowing you to identify yourself and leave a reference back to your blog. Anonymous comments will obviously not do this!

Comments like "I agree" are close to worthless. Also, your comments must not be seen as commercial. It's important not to jump in and mention products or solutions that involve you or your company. No matter how well intentioned, it's easy to be seen as inappropriately self-promoting. In many ways, comments must be written more carefully than blog posts! You can always modify or delete a blog post you wrote, but a comment on someone else's blog is beyond your control. If you regret leaving a comment, there is little you can do other than perhaps politely asking to have it removed.

Link to Other Blogs' Posts

We mentioned using trackbacks as a promotional technique in the last chapter. Sometimes you can't use trackbacks because they are not universally implemented. If you want to refer to and comment on another blogger's post from your blog, it is simple enough to link to that post and then write your comments.

Most bloggers do not have extensive links, so they will find your link, perhaps through Technorati, PubSub, or Google Blog Search. Simple curiosity will force them to visit your site to see who linked and what you said. Because they obviously had content that interested you, it's quite possible that they will be interested in your content as well. Even if you disagree and offer a dissenting opinion, you obviously have common interests.

OTHER PROMOTIONAL TECHNIQUES

Blog Traffic Exchanges

Blog traffic exchanges send visitors to your blog in exchange for you visiting other blogs. There is rarely a fee to join. They normally send one visitor for each two blogs you visit, with some minimum visit time, usually around 20 to 30 seconds. There are numerous variants of traffic exchanges, which all operate somewhat differently. Some blog traffic exchanges include Blog Explosion, blog advance, BlogClicker, and many more.

Blog traffic exchanges work, but the traffic they send can be low quality and unfocused. The best blog traffic exchanges break blogs into different categories such as business, technology, political, etc., and allow users to visit the types of blogs in which they are interested. The result is more focused traffic. Many blog traffic exchanges also sell inexpensive advertising and traffic; traffic can cost less than one cent per visitor and can result in some regular readers. Many blog traffic exchanges also have associated blog directories.

Ping-o-Matic

Ping-o-Matic, http://www.pingomatic.com, is a free service that automatically lets many services know when you've updated your blog. These include some search engines such as Feedster, Blog-digger, and Technorati, as well as services that maintain lists of recently updated blogs such as weblogs.com and blo.gs, and blog-roll services such as blogrolling.com that list most recently updated blogs first. Ping-o-Matic is run manually after you add or edit a post and will help get your new content noticed and indexed more quickly.

Too-Good-to-Be-True Traffic Building Techniques

It is very common to see offers that seem too good to be true, especially on the Internet. The rule that if it seems too good to be true it is still holds especially on the Internet. You didn't just win a massive sweepstakes you never entered, no one is going to give you an absurd amount of money for helping someone overseas in distress, and you cannot get massive traffic to your blog or Web site for a few dollars and negligible effort.

Some incredible claims of creating massive Internet traffic do work. They typically use "tricks" to fool the search engines, at least in the short term; however, the search engines keep getting smarter. Not only do tricks usually stop working after a while, but Web sites and blogs can and do get banned from search engine results. One mutual friend of Shel and Ted's used one such scheme. He had enormous search engine traffic for a while. Now his Web site has been banned from Google for over a year, even though he has long since stopped using this technique. Other search engines do send him traffic, but Google still does not. It's not worth the risk; if it seems too good to be true, it is.

PROMOTING AN INTRANET BLOG

In one sense, promoting a new blog on an intranet—targeting employees and not for distribution outside the company—is no different that introducing any new employee resource. You need to make it clear to employees why they should pay attention to the blog by explaining how it relates to their jobs and how it will help them. Any approach to raising awareness in the workplace can be applied to a blog launch, including print collateral (like posters and cafeteria table tent cards), intranet home page visibility, and verbal references in face-to-face sessions such as town hall meetings.

A CEO blog isn't likely to need much marketing. That the CEO is engaging in a dialogue with employees through a blog is news that should spread pretty quickly without much need for a push. But considering the number of uses to which blogs can be put internally, getting the word to the right audience can be difficult. Imagine, for instance, a blog dedicated to daily reporting of the goings-on in a project team. Every employee interested in progress on the project would benefit from checking the blog (or its Web feed), but these employees are spread throughout the organization. How could you reach them all when you don't even know who all of them are?

Some of the means of keeping employees advised of blog launches that would interest them are similar to techniques you would apply to external blog marketing:

- Make sure links to the blog appear on pages related to the theme of the blog. A project blog for the Super Widget

Product Development team should be accessible from all the pages that deal with the Super Widget project.

- Maintain a master list of intranet blogs, just as Sun Microsystems and Thomas Nelson Publishers maintain lists on their Web sites of all their external blogs.
- Offer blogrolls, commenting, and Web feeds.

Beyond these techniques, however, there are some additional steps you can take that are more suited to intranets than blogs on the World Wide Web:

- Create an e-mail mailing list and Web feed dedicated to announcements of new intranet blogs.
- Include new blog launches in your regular reporting mechanisms. If you produce a weekly e-mail newsletter, for example, add a section covering the week's new blog launches.
- Create a community for intranet bloggers where they can connect with one another over problems, ideas, and issues. This could be a wiki, a message board, or even a group blog. Bringing together the community of bloggers will lead individuals to learn of other blogs they might otherwise have never seen.

SUMMARY

We've looked at a number of ways to promote your blog. We start with the premise that your blog is worth promoting; that it has good material. Good posts, as well as a reasonable look and feel, are essential. The best promotional techniques will not help a poor blog much!

We've also considered other blog promotional techniques. Different techniques will appeal to and be used by different people. Some bloggers like leaving copious comments on other blogs;

others do not. Some bloggers may not want to include their blog information in their e-mail signatures. Use the techniques that you feel would work best for you and your organization.

In the next chapter, we'll look at search engine optimization techniques. Even if used somewhat modestly and sparingly, search engine optimization can help increase the number of new visitors significantly.

10

USING SEARCH ENGINES
TO PROMOTE YOUR BLOG

Search engine optimization, or SEO as it's popularly called, is the process of optimizing Web content so that search engines will rank it highly. This is important as search engines can be significant sources of new traffic, and some of that traffic will result in regular readers and potential business. There is an entire service industry built around SEO. Fortunately, blogs are search engine friendly by default, yet some judicious SEO can bring more readers from the search engines. In fact, blogging alone is a very effective SEO technique, and blogging, together with its links, will elevate you in the search engines.

SEO can be divided into two areas, sometimes called ethical SEO and unethical SEO, or whitehat SEO and blackhat SEO. Ethical SEO includes optimizing your content and letting search engines know about your pages—essentially helping search engines do a good job. Unethical SEO just doesn't pay. It includes creating a lot of spam links to your pages and hiding text with popularly searched terms such as *sex* in your content—essentially trying to cheat or fool the search engines. We will be discussing only ethical SEO techniques in this chapter for several reasons, the most important of which is that unethical SEO techniques can result in your entire site being banned from the search engines, giving you and your organization an "unethical" reputation!

ISN'T WRITING GOOD CONTENT ENOUGH?

You can go overboard and spend endless time on the SEO techniques on which we will touch. You can even go back and reoptimize old posts based on newer keywords, search engine algorithms, and Web searching trends.

Isn't writing good content enough? Writing good content is necessary, but not sufficient. Although writing good content may be the most important thing from the search engine perspective, it does absolutely no good if the search engine never indexes you, or if people are searching using the term *dog food* and your blog content uses the term *doggie dinner*. There is a lot of good content out there, and much of it gets buried in the search engine results pages. Sometimes making a few minor changes and considerations will significantly change search engine rankings and resultant visitors.

MOVING TARGET

Search engines are certainly not perfect, but they work well and are improving rapidly. They are constantly refining their techniques and methods, so SEO techniques and "tricks" that work today might not work tomorrow. We are concentrating on techniques that should not change, at least not rapidly. Tried and tested approaches that help the search engines do a better job of categorizing material, help searchers by returning more relevant information, and help content providers such as Web site administrators and bloggers should not change soon.

In general, search engines categorize information by constantly searching the Web via programs called "crawlers" or "spiders." It's also believed that some of the search engines also employ human editors who read pages and help determine how they are rated by search engines. Optimization tricks and unethical techniques may fool an automated program but are unlikely to fool a human.

SEO IS A "BEST GUESS"

Search engines' algorithms, besides evolving and changing regularly, are kept secret on purpose! The search engines want to concentrate on returning the best content for searches, not returning the content that was optimized best to their current algorithms. SEO experts often disagree on SEO techniques. SEO in many ways is a best guess of what will work. We have concentrated on relatively noncontroversial techniques below, but beware that even SEO professionals will differ on the relative merits of the techniques we discuss.

TIPS FOR SPECIFIC SEARCH ENGINES

General Purpose Search Engines

Many general purpose search engines—for example, Google—will allow you to request a page to be crawled to their databases. Normally, only the blog's main page needs to be added and the additional pages will be discovered automatically. It can take several weeks to months for the search engine spiders to get around to indexing your blog for the first time! However, if you can get any inbound links—links from other sites to your blog as discussed later in this chapter—a spider crawling these links will index your blog more quickly. Consequently, the linking nature of blogs can enhance the chances that your blog will be found.

Submitting your blog's main page to the search engines that have this functionality is a reasonable approach. It is not necessary, but may result in the search engines finding your blog more quickly, and it cannot hurt. Do not do this repeatedly, however; that is, do not spam the search engines. It can hurt if you violate their unwritten policies! Just submit your blog once, and only submit the main page. If you feel it is necessary, you can repeat this process after a month or so with no ill effects. You can add your blog to Google at http://www.google.com/addurl/?continue=/addurl, and to MSN at http://beta.search.msn.com/docs/submit.aspx.

There are also paid services that will submit your URLs to the various search engines. You may want to research and consider these, but quite frankly they are unnecessary for blogs.

Blog-Specific Search Engines

Technorati. The extremely popular Technorati—the self-described authority on what's going on in the world of Web logs—allows users to create a free account and "claim" their Web log. Claiming your blog will get it into the Technorati search database quickly and is recommended. Depending on your blog software, this may involve adding a small section of Technorati-specific code to your blog's template that proves ownership.

We discussed Technorati tags previously. They allow applying simple category or subject descriptions to blog posts, as well as links and photos. Technorati allows searching on tags.

Tags are not predefined but can be chosen on the fly, and blogging software that supports categories will automatically include tag information in the RSS or Atom feed. Users of blog software that doesn't support categories and RSS/Atom feeds can still use tags by adding a small piece of code that defines a link to the HTML of a blog post. For example, the following code added to a blog post tags it as "dogs," a popular tag name.

```
<a href="http://technorati.com/tag/dogs" rel= "tag">dogs</a>
```

Technorati can display the most popular tags, which can be useful for helping choose tags for your blog posts. Ted does not currently tag his posts. Shel does, via his blogging software's support for categories. (See Figure 10.1.)

FIGURE 10.1 *Technorati Tags*

Source: Technorati (www.technorati.com).

Google Blog Search. Google Blog Search is an RSS/Atom search engine (RSS/Atom search engines are discussed below); however, because Google is considered the 800-pound gorilla of search engines we discuss it separately.

Most modern blog software automatically pings at least one updating service like Weblogs.com or blo.gs when updated. These free services maintain lists of recently updated blogs. If your blog software does ping them, Google Blog Search will automatically find it. Another way to ping them is via http://pingomatic.com. Google will also provide a form for manually adding your blog to their index in the future.

Daypop, RSS/Atom search engines, and others. Daypop will allow you to submit blogs at http://www.daypop.com/info/submit .htm, although there is no guarantee it will index you. It is only interested in blogs that update and provide information on a timely basis.

There are a number of directories where you can submit RSS and Atom feeds. This is a nonexhaustive list of relatively established feed directories, which will presumably still exist when you read this. A search for "RSS directory" from a general purpose search engine will find many more. If you don't add your feed, your blog may or may not eventually get added.

Name	Feed format	URL pathname for adding blogs
Feedster.com	Atom/RSS	http://feedster.com/add.php
Blogdigger.com	Atom/RSS	http://blogdigger.com/add.jsp
2RSS.com	RSS	http://2rss.com
icerocket.com	Atom/RSS	http://www.icerocket.com/ c?p=addblog

OPTIMIZATION CONCEPTS AND TECHNIQUES

We'll look at the most important concepts and techniques for blog SEO, including choosing and using good keywords and phrases, post lengths, meta tags and the title tag, and incoming links. This is not intended as an inclusive list; entire books can be written on SEO, although they would no doubt be out of date by the time they were finished. The emphasis here is on simple techniques that work and should not change quickly.

Keywords and Phrases

Keywords are very simply what the term suggests they are—words that are important to your material and that searchers use to find your blog. For example, a post on vegetarian dog food and a dog's health would include the keywords *vegetarian, dog, food,* and *health.* A post on wireless access and security would include the keywords *wireless, access,* and *security.* Complete phrases are important as well because people may be searching using phrases such as *vegetarian dog* and *wireless security.*

It is important to choose the right keywords. Suppose you had a blog about dogs and you were writing about vegetarian dog food, which you believe is great for dogs. If you used the phrase *vegetarian dog food* in your writing, and otherwise optimized for that phrase, as we'll be discussing, you might think you would get a lot of traffic from people looking for vegetarian dog food. You probably would, but you'd be missing a larger group of people searching for *premium dog food* or *healthy dog food.* If the vegetarian dog food you were writing about were also premium dog food, including that phrase in your post or post title would be a great idea from the SEO perspective. Adding the term *healthy dog food* to your keywords may bring even more targeted traffic. *Dog treat* is a popular search term as well, and you may want to include that phrase if appropriate. Presumably, *vegetarian dog food* will bring you more focused traffic than *premium dog food,* which in turn will bring in more focused traffic than *dog treat,* but people searching for all those terms are potentially interested in what you have to say about vegetarian dog food. They may also become regular readers of your blog and eventually customers.

There are several tools available that provide information about keyword and key phrase popularity. A search using the term *keywords* will uncover several services, both free and paid. Perhaps the two most popular are wordtracker.com, which is a pay service although it offers a free trial, and Overture's Keyword Selector Tool, which is free. It can currently be found at http://inventory .overture.com/d/searchinventory/suggestion/.

So, what do you do with keywords and phrases? You use them in your text in a natural and reasonable fashion, and place them in a few other important places. Let's look at a number of places where keywords and phrases should go.

Title. The title (or headline) of your post should be as descriptive as possible. In other words, it should contain keywords and phrases. Ideally, they should be the first words in your title. In our example of vegetarian dog food, poor titles would include:

Good for your dog!
Feed your dog right.

Notice the lack of your keywords and phrases. Here is a much better title from the SEO perspective:

Vegetarian dog food is good for your dog

Logically, a post about vegetarian dog food should contain the phrase *vegetarian dog food* in the title, and the search engines agree.

If appropriate for the post, the following two titles are better:

Vegetarian dog food and dog treats
Premium dog food: vegetarian dog food is great!

They both have the phrase *vegetarian dog food* and the additional phrases *dog treats* and *premium dog food.*

Text of your post. Your keywords and phrases need to be in the text of your post as high up in the text as possible and preferably repeated a few times in a natural fashion. Don't sacrifice readability of your post to "cram" more keywords in! If your content is good and your keywords appropriate, they can naturally occur repeatedly in your content.

Consider the following initial text of a post about vegetarian dog food. Notice that your most important phase, *vegetarian dog food,* doesn't even occur until the second paragraph!

Example 1:
So, you want to do what's best for your dog. You take him to the vet regularly. Take him for walks every morning and night and play with him as much as possible. Give him good food. Make sure he always has fresh water to drink and toys to play with. Get together with other dog owners so he can play with other dogs.
Have you ever thought much about his diet? Sure, you buy a "name brand" dog food, but how good is it really? Feeding your dog vegetarian dog food is one of the healthiest . . .

We've slightly rewritten this text to make it more search engine friendly:

Example 2:
So, you want to do what's best for your dog. You feed him premium dog food. You take him to the vet regularly. Take him

for walks and play with him often. Make sure he always has fresh water to drink and toys to play with. Get together with other dog owners so he can play with other dogs.

Have you ever thought about feeding him vegetarian dog food? Sure, you buy a "name brand" dog food, but how good is it really? Feeding your dog vegetarian dog food is one of the healthiest. . .

Notice that we have a key phrase, *premium dog food*, in the first line of the post now. *Vegetarian dog food* appears slightly higher and it naturally repeats. Although improved, it would be significantly better if we could rewrite it to have *vegetarian dog food* appear in the first or second sentence.

Maybe we don't want to rewrite it. Perhaps we like the style in which it's written, or have more important things to do than obsess over SEO details. One simple technique is to use a subtitle, which appears at the beginning of the text, that includes keywords and phrases.

If we used the title "Premium dog food: vegetarian dog food is great!" for our post title, we might use the subtitle shown below:

Example 3:

Vegetarian dog food is among the best premium dog food around!

So, you want to do what's best for your dog. You feed him premium dog food. You take him to the vet regularly. Take him for walks and play with him often. Make sure he always has fresh water to drink and toys to play with. Get together with other dog owners so he can play with other dogs.

Have you ever thought about feeding him vegetarian dog food?? Sure, you buy a "name brand" dog food, but how good is it really? Feeding your dog vegetarian dog food is one of the healthiest . . .

Notice we haven't rewritten the text; we just added a subtitle, and in doing so, added two key phrases, *vegetarian dog food* and *premium dog food* to the first line of our post!

Of course you can go overboard. Look at the nonsense below:

Example 4:

Vegetarian dog food is among the best premium dog food around!

Vegetarian dog food and dog treats are the best premium dog food. All informed dog owners must feed their dogs vegetarian dog food and dog treats.

Have you ever thought about feeding your dog premium dog food which is vegetarian dog food?? Feeding your dog vegetarian dog food and vegetarian dog treats is very healthy! Vegetarian dog food and dog treats will help your dog have a healthy coat. Dogs that eat vegetarian dog food and vegetarian dog treats are happy and long lived! . . .

It's awkward and obtuse. Your readers won't like it, and the search engines probably won't either because the *keyword density,* a popular SEO term, is unnatural, as is the entire post.

Headings and heading tags. Web sites and blogs are written in HTML as we've mentioned, although many bloggers never see or edit the HTML code directly. HTML allows the use of heading tags to specify the size of headers. Heading tags range from heading one to heading six, although anything beyond heading one and heading two are rarely used in posts.

Search engines assume that if text is in a heading, it must be important, which makes headings an ideal location to place keywords or phrases. Headings one through six are defined in HTML with the tags <h1> to <h6>. Using example 3 from above, we could define the subheading as heading one, emphasizing the keywords and phrases to the search engines.

Example 3 in HTML:

<h1>Vegetarian dog food is among the best premium dog food around!</h1>

So, you want to do what's best for your dog. You feed him premium dog food. You take him to the vet regularly. Take him for walks and play with him often. Make sure he always has fresh water to drink and toys to play with. Get together with other dog owners so he can play with other dogs.

Have you ever thought about feeding him vegetarian dog food?? Sure, you buy a "name brand" dog food, but how good is it really? Feeding your dog vegetarian dog food is one of the healthiest . . .

Notice in Figure 10.2 that heading one appears in a large bold font in a browser window.

Heading one is in a larger font than heading two, which is in a larger font than heading three, etc. We show an example of headings one through four in the screenshot in Figure 10.3.

If the size of the heading is not to your liking—for example, it is much too large—it is possible to change the heading by modifying your template.

FIGURE 10.2 *Heading One Appears in a Larger Font*

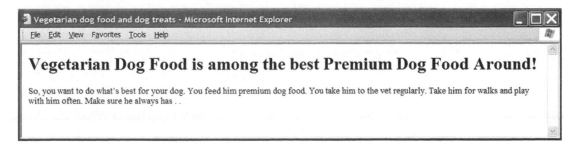

FIGURE 10.3 *Typical Heading One through Heading Four Font Sizes*

Browser window titled "Vegetarian dog food and dog treats - ..." showing:

This is h1 text

This is h2 text

This is h3 text

This is h4 text

Alt image tags. If you use graphics in your blog, you can designate an alternative text that describes the content of the image. This text is displayed while the graphics are loading, and can be used by the sight-impaired to help navigate your blog or Web site. Some programs allow you to easily add so-called "alt descriptions," but it is also simple to do it manually via HTML. The following section of HTML code displays the graphics file "eatingdogs .jpg" for our hypothetical post about vegetarian dog food. The width and height parameters describe the image size in pixels.

```
<img src="eatingdogs.jpg" width="144" height="120">
```

We can add a keyword description of the image very simply by adding an "alt" attribute as shown below.

```
<img src="eatingdogs.jpg" alt="Vegetarian Dog Food: Dogs love it!"
width="144" height="120">
```

Many people would also recommend giving the file that contains the graphics a keyword-rich name also. You could rename the file "eatingdogs.html" to "vegetarian-dog-food.jpg" instead. Hyphens are suggested by many SEO experts for separating words in file names. For highly competitive searches, every little bit can help.

```
<img src=" vegetarian-dog-food.jpg " alt="Vegetarian Dog Food:
Dogs love it!" width="144" height="120">
```

Links. Where appropriate, links can contain keywords. Rather than saying, "Here is a link to a related article," it would be far better to say, "I recommend this article on vegetarian dog food." Keywords in links have more relevance to search engines than ordinary text.

Post Length

Does the length of a post or Web page matter to the search engines? There is a general consensus that to successfully be ranked highly by search engines, your pages need to include a minimum useful amount of content, and 250 words is an often-quoted minimum length. Obviously many blog posts are much shorter, but you should try to have a few paragraphs of naturally keyword-rich content in important posts.

Meta Tags and Title

Recall that HTML describes to a browser how to display a Web page, whether it's a part of a blog or anything else. So far we have been looking at how to optimize a blog post for SEO by concentrating on the information that is in the body of an HTML document and what appears on a Web page of the blog, as shown below.

```
<html

<head>
<!-- header information about this document, which is NOT dis-
played on the page -->
</head>

<body>

<!-- the HTML for display --> .
    .
    .
</body>

</html>
```

There is also information that goes into the header of a HTML document that can influence search engines. The "main" or "home" page of a blog will be described as an HTML document. Usually each post will also be saved as an individual HTML document/ Web page by default; some blogging software is configurable in this regard. There are usually archive pages as well, accessible from the sidebar, which contain all the posts by month or week. For SEO purposes, we want each post to be available as a separate page, and in the following discussion we will assume that each separate HTML document/Web page is stored as a separate file.

There are three things we can place or modify in the header that will affect search engines. They are the title tag, the meta description tag, and the meta keywords tag. Let's look at an example, then discuss them, and look at how they are commonly and practically used by blogs. Note that the order is not syntactically important, although most SEO experts prefer that the title comes first.

```
<html>
    <head>
    <title>The Ted Rap</title>
    <meta name="description" content="Ted Demopoulos'
    thoughts and musings on information technology, security,
    business, and more">
    <meta name="keywords" content="Ted Demopoulos,
    speaker,consulting,training,technology,business,information
    technology,IT,security,business,businessimplications,information
    security,enterprise security">
```

The title tag. The title tag is very important to search engines. The title tag contains the title of the Web page and shows up in the top of most browsers' windows. Most blog software will automatically set the title tag for a blog's main page, post pages, and archive pages to something at least semi-intelligent. It's common for blog software to default to setting the main page to the blog's name, the archive page to some variant of the blog's name such as the name and date, and the post pages to the title of the post, perhaps with the blog's name as well.

```
<title>The Ted Rap</title>
```

The example above is from the main page of The Ted Rap blog. It is simply the blog's name, which is the default setting in Blogger. Ted could have a much better title if he included keywords. For example:

```
<title>Information Technology, Security, Business: The Ted Rap</title>
```

Making this modification to Ted's blog involved modifying his blog's template.

The description and keywords tags. These tags are not as important as they used to be because some search engines, such as Google, are widely believed to not look at them anymore.

The description tag is exactly that: a description about what the Web page contains. Some search engines use this description when returning search results. This is very useful because you can control what users see when your blog is included in search engine results, and a compelling description can encourage them to visit.

The keywords tag contains keywords. It is important not to spam the search engines by placing popular yet unrelated keywords or multiple copies of the same keyword in the keywords tag. Some search engines prefer to determine the keywords themselves, but other search engines do consider the contents of the keywords tag.

Most blogging software does not automatically set the description and keywords tags. Because they are not overly important, many bloggers never worry about it. They are worth setting, however, because every bit helps, and some search engines do consider them. Very few blogs seem to set them differently for the main, archive, and post pages. Most set them just once globally, if at all. This can easily be done by modifying a blog's template and adding them.

Domain Names and URLs

Especially important keywords can sometimes be part of a blog's domain name or URL. If our blog concentrates on vegetarian dog food, then vegetariandogfood.com would be an excellent domain name for your blog. If your first choice is taken (perhaps not surprisingly, vegetariandogfood.com is not available), try a similar choice such as vegetarian-dog-food.com or vegetariandogfood.org; premiumdogfood.com and dogfood.com would be good choices too, if available.

Quite often you won't have the flexibility of choosing a new domain name for your blog. It may be part of a hosted solution, or hosted on the main company's Web site, for example. An option might be having a blog URL similar to vegetariandogfood.*hosting company*.com, vegetariandogfood.*companyname*.com, or *companyname*.com/vegetariandogfood.

INBOUND LINKS

Every link from another Web site to yours is seen as an endorsement by the search engines. As Web sites and blogs tend to link to useful and valuable content, this certainly makes sense. Links from external sites are extremely important in determining search engine ranks and some SEO professionals would say they are the most important factor in achieving high rankings.

Not all links are created equal. Links from a high-ranked site are worth more than links from a low-ranked site. Links with keywords in the link text are especially valuable. A link that says "check this out" from a brand new blog is not particularly valuable; however, a link to your blog that contains keywords from an established, well-regarded, and popular site is worth much more.

Links from a Company's Web Site

There should be links from the company's Web site or Web sites, even if the blog is under the same domain name. Certainly some people will follow the links to find your blog. Also, if the company's Web site is known to the search engines and regularly crawled, the search engines will follow this link and catalog the blog fairly quickly.

Links from Blog Directories

There are a lot of blog directories and many in existence today will not be by the time you read this! Blog directories' entries typically do not create a lot of traffic, but they create valuable inbound links. This is especially important for new blogs because some of these directories are crawled by the search engines often and will cause your blog to be discovered and catalogued more quickly. A search for the term *blog directory* will return many. We hate to give any specific recommendations as they may be obsolete quickly; however, the following four are good places to start because the search engines seem to visit them very often: Eaton Web, Blog Explosion, Globe of Blogs, and Blog Rankings. Registration in blog directories is usually free and easy.

Links to Your Posts

Bloggers (and others) often link to other bloggers' posts and comment on them. They might link to agree with the posts, to disagree with them, or simply because they like the posts and think their readers will benefit from them. This is another case in which writing great content is important! The better content you have, the more likely that others will link to it.

There is nothing wrong with sending someone an e-mail, whether they are a blogger or not, alerting them about a post you've written that you think they might find useful or enjoy. Be careful not to overdo it, however, and be seen as spamming them!

Links in Trackbacks

Recall that trackbacks really are just comments left on another blog. If your blog and the blog you want to comment on both implement trackbacks, this is a great way to get inbound links. Every time you comment on someone's post on your blog and use trackbacks, there is a link created from their blog to yours. It is extremely important to not abuse trackbacks; make sure you are writing a legitimate comment that adds value. Otherwise, you may find your trackback deleted or refused if the blog is using trackback moderation.

Links in Articles

Many blog posts are essentially miniarticles, and with little work can be turned into formal articles. Many Web sites are happy to have your article and give you a link back to your Web site or blog in return; many Webmasters are always looking for good content.

One way to do this is to submit these articles to article directories. Article directories will make your article available online with an author byline that includes a link. Usually anyone is allowed to copy and use your article, perhaps online or in an e-zine/newsletter, as long as they leave your author byline, including links, intact. Some popular article directories include: EzineArticles, ArticleCity, and GoArticles. Be sure to check the terms of service and any other required agreements.

There is a downside to this. Search engines may rank copies of your articles higher than your original blog posts, redirecting search engine traffic away from your blog. Also, some search engines, such as Google, frown on duplicate content. This can cause your original posts to be ignored or downgraded by some search engines, as well as reduce the value of incoming links from multiple copies of your articles. It is still a valuable technique to consider, however.

Links in Blogrolls

We've discussed blogrolls in depth before. Blogrolls can be good sources of incoming links, especially if from more established and popular blogs.

Links in Advertisements

Blogs can advertise. There are plenty of Web sites and blogs that sell advertisements. From the SEO perspective, an advertisement is far more than just an advertisement because it will contain a keyword-rich link that can increase search engine rankings. This is especially important because sites selling advertisements tend to be highly regarded by search engines, and their prices usually reflect their popularity. An advertisement is, at least in part, buying a link.

However, remember that the link goes away when you stop advertising, unlike links gained from organic sources, such as other bloggers adding you to their blogrolls and sites linking to your posts.

SEO FOR BLOGS VERSUS WEB SITES

SEO for blogs and Web sites is essentially the same. A search engine doesn't care if a page it is crawling is part of a blog or Web site. For many Web sites, SEO is critical. They live or die based on their traffic from new visitors, much of which needs to come from search engines. Alternatively, some Web sites are essentially online alternatives or supplements to a company's printed brochure, and traffic is not important. Most Web sites have fewer pages than a typical blog and new information is added far less frequently; consequently, more effort can be spent optimizing the content of Web sites for search engines.

HOW MUCH SHOULD YOU DO?

Few bloggers spend as much time tweaking each post and detail of their blog as Webmasters do. It simply is extremely time-consuming and blogs have a lot of content, with new content often added every day. It is possible to fall into the "SEO trap" and spend more time on SEO than on writing new material!

Blogs by design are already search engine friendly. Because they are expected to have new content added often, because bloggers often link to each other, and for other reasons that probably only the search engines understand, they tend to be crawled and indexed by the search engines fairly frequently. It's quite common for a blog post to suddenly start appearing in the first page of search engine results a few days after it's written.

A little bit of SEO can make a blog even more search engine friendly. At a minimum, try to use descriptive post titles with appropriate keywords. Create good content, with appropriate keywords included in a natural fashion. You may occasionally want to check keyword popularity for particularly important posts; perhaps you will find a slightly different but similar keyword or phrase that is much more popular. For example, maybe *training* is more popular than *seminar,* or *crushed stone* more popular than *gravel.* If either word is appropriate and natural, the more popular one may be a better choice; use your judgment! Above all, create the best content you can and don't obsess over SEO for your blog!

SUMMARY

Now that you've promoted your blog and made it search engine friendly, how do you know if it's effective? How do you even know if anyone is reading it? Having a blog is great, but unless you can measure its effectiveness, you may not be reaping its full benefits. By tapping into the wealth of services available on the World Wide Web—many of them free and easy to use—you can ensure your efforts are reaching your intended audience. That's the topic of the next chapter.

11

MEASURING THE RESULTS OF YOUR BLOG

Beyond the time it takes to manage them, blogs don't represent a huge investment of time, and it may be tempting to bypass any measurement of the effectiveness of your efforts. In fact, it's surprising how many organizations don't have formal processes to measure their traditional communications. With blogs, though, the return on investment may seem obvious. You don't, after all, measure the effectiveness of a telephone system for your company. You don't need to, because it's painfully clear how difficult it would be to run your business *without* telephones. After a while, if you've implemented a solid blogging program, blogs could come to seem as irreplaceable as phones.

There are good reasons to take the time and effort to assess how your blogging efforts are performing based on your goals. It is paramount to determine if you're doing it correctly. Even if your results are good, research could well reveal a variety of ways of doing it *better*.

Blogs are a new enough phenomenon, however, that measurement models have not evolved to the extent to which you are able to measure more traditional communications. Still, because of the direct interaction blogs provide, measuring a blog's effectiveness can, in some ways, be easier than measuring a traditional PR, advertising, or marketing campaign.

SERVER STATISTICS

The server on which your blog is installed automatically cranks out the easiest measurement to obtain: Web log statistics.

Confused? The word *blog*, after all, is a shortened version of the term *Web log*, which is what we've been talking about in this book. But Web log has a second, completely different meaning as well. A Web log is the record your Web server maintains for every request it receives to deliver Web content. By using software that interprets this raw data and displays it in a way that's easy to understand—WebTrends, for example—you can figure out how many people are looking at your blog, what pages they're reading, where they came from, and a variety of other types of information.

In fact, free services are available that will keep you from having to install anything on your server. For example, My.StatCounter .com provides detailed statistics when you enroll for a free account and provide the URL of the page you want tracked.

The screen shot in Figure 11.1 shows the various statistics that you can access using My.StatCounter.com. The default screen displays total page loads and then splits them between new and returning visitors. Other options include the most popular pages visited on your blog, the paths your visitors have followed, where they came from (for example, if they came from a Google search or a link on another blog post), and the keywords a visitor used to find your blog.

If your blog is hosted by a commercial service, you probably have access to detailed statistics. Many hosting services provide

FIGURE 11.1 *StatCounter Reports Traffic to Your Site, Distinguishing between New and Returning Readers*

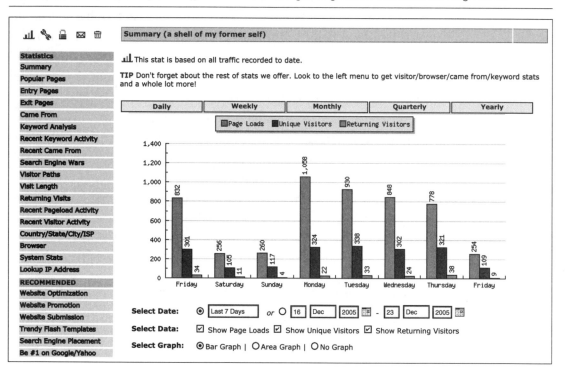

users with WebTrends statistics, the same Web analysis software many corporations install on their Web servers.

MEASURING FEEDS

Not all of your readers will necessarily retrieve an actual page of your blog from your Web server. As syndication grows and the ability to "subscribe" to content becomes easier, more and more people will use RSS newsreaders (or "aggregators") to read your blog. Offering a link to "subscribe" to your blog is a great way to connect with your readers and keep them current when you post new content. You need to be able to measure these subscriptions to your feed in order to accurately track circulation.

Your server will record pings to your feed, but these hits may come from a wide variety of aggregators that each poll for content differently on behalf of one or many individuals, making it difficult to gauge individual subscribers. With thousands of aggregators on the market, your Web server statistics are not an accurate measurement of subscribers to your feed.

There are services available that make it easy to track circulation, click-throughs, item popularity, aggregator types, and other useful data. By directing subscriptions to your feed through a service like FeedBurner, you can track subscriber information in one place. FeedBurner works on behalf of bloggers, podcasters, and anyone who publishes a feed to help measure audience size and growth, extend subscriber reach, and optimize delivery of your content to various endpoints like mobile phones or PDAs. (See Figure 11.2.)

FIGURE 11.2 *Feedburner Displays the Number of Subscribers to Each of the Blogs You Maintain in Your Feedburner Account*

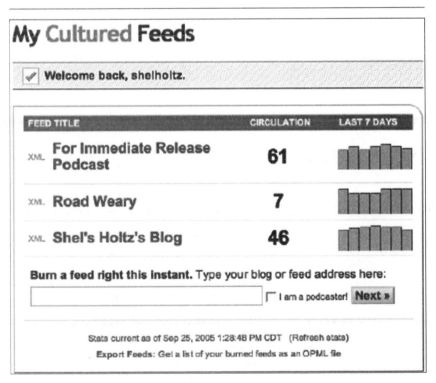

As you can see, Shel's account shows 61 Feedburner subscribers for his podcast blog, 46 for his primary blog, and seven for his travel blog. By selecting one blog, you can drill deeper into statistics. By selecting the "readership" tab, for example, you can find out what newsreaders your readers are using. (See Figure 11.3.)

Other services exist that can provide more detail, but you'll have to pay for them. For example, Syndicate IQ, http://www.syndicateiq .com, will measure the growth of subscribers, individual feed subscriptions, and a feed's average daily readership (ADR). And Nooked, http://www.nooked.com, is a company that will manage your RSS feeds on its own servers, including the ability to track click-throughs, subscriptions, daily trends, RSS click-through rates (RCTR), and customer content preferences.

FIGURE 11.3 *Feedburner Offers a Variety of Views of Your Subscription Data*

Burn This! - The FeedBurner Weblog   🔥 FeedBurner™
(http://feeds.feedburner.com/BurnThisRSS2)

Edit Feed Details... | Delete Feed...

| **Analyze** | Optimize | Publicize | Monetize | Troubleshootize | 🏠 My Feeds |

↓ VIEW

ıl Feed Circulation

🕲 Readership

🗋 Item Stats

↓ SERVICES

✓ StandardStats

✓ TotalStats **PRO**

? Stats Terms Explained...

Feed Originally Burned On:
Feb 29, 2004 9:03 PM

Do you have an interesting story to tell? Contact us to become a FeedBurner case study.

Feed Live Circulation: 5,636

Set Reporting Range: [Earliest to Date ⬍] (Update)

Daily Circulation Trend   **PRO** Feature Enhanced
(Feb 29, 2004 - Nov 17, 2005)

Display as: 🗠 Chart | ▦ Table   Export this data as: Excel | CSV

Circulation: 6,000 / 4,000 / 2,000 / 0

Apr-2004 Jul-2004 Oct-2004 Jan-2005 Apr-2005 Jul-2005 Oct-2005

Reporting Range

ACTUAL REVENUES AND SITE TRAFFIC

A blog that blatantly sells products or services is not going to sit well with the blog-reading community. Still, you could subtly place an offer in your blog. For example, Steve Rubel, author of the popular PR-focused Micro Persuasion blog, offered his readers a free month of NetFlix service; the DVD rental service provided Rubel with the link and was able to measure directly how many new subscribers came from Rubel's blog, and then how many of those made the transition from the free month to paying customer.

Traffic to content on your traditional Web site also can be driven by your blog. For example, a post to your blog may contain a link to related content on your Web site, such as a current promotion. When Web hosting company GoDaddy produced a controversial commercial for the Super Bowl, a blog post about the controversy included a link to the commercial on the firm's Web site, resulting in considerable extra traffic to view the commercial. And, of course, that traffic is measurable.

SEARCH ENGINE RANKINGS

Organizations invest a substantial amount of money to improve their ability to be found by search engines such as Google, Yahoo!, and MSN Search. These search engines rank sites based on content they find when they crawl the Web, sending out software agents called spiders to index every word on every page they can find. Blogs—looked at as Web pages by the spiders—are included in the material crawled by the search engines. The mere presence of the blog will enable somebody conducting a search to find it; its ranking will increase every time somebody links to it via trackback or even just a link from a post on another blog.

From a measurement standpoint, you could determine how your content is turning up in search engines and assign a dollar amount based on what it would cost to achieve those kinds of results with the help of a search engine optimization consultant.

ASSESSING COMMENTS

Content analysis is one of the age-old tools of the public relations business. In a simple content analysis, you determine the percentage of source material that is positive, neutral, and negative. Once you know these percentages, it becomes a relatively easy matter to track movement of opinion from negative into the neutral and positive categories.

For example, let's assume a company experiences a product recall. Using the blog where the company has built a following and a store of goodwill, the blog's author begins writing about the recall. He provides an ongoing narrative about the company's compliance with the recall order and its efforts to redress the situation. Initially, comments are highly critical. But the blog continues to offer insights into the company's efforts, satisfying customer demands for transparency and sincerity, and gradually the tone of the comments begins to shift. With the first post, perhaps 80 percent of the comments were negative, but after a few days that number has dropped to 65 percent, with 10 percent moving into the neutral category and 5 percent into the positive. A few days more and most comments are either positive or neutral. And, of course, everybody who reads the comments is influenced by the support the company's rehabilitation efforts have garnered.

In addition to reading comments, some blogging utilities allow you to add polls to your posts. Using a poll, you can ask your readers to respond to a specific question after they have read a post. (See Figure 11.4.)

FIGURE 11.4 *A Poll Added to a Post at the OracleApps Blog*

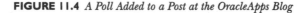

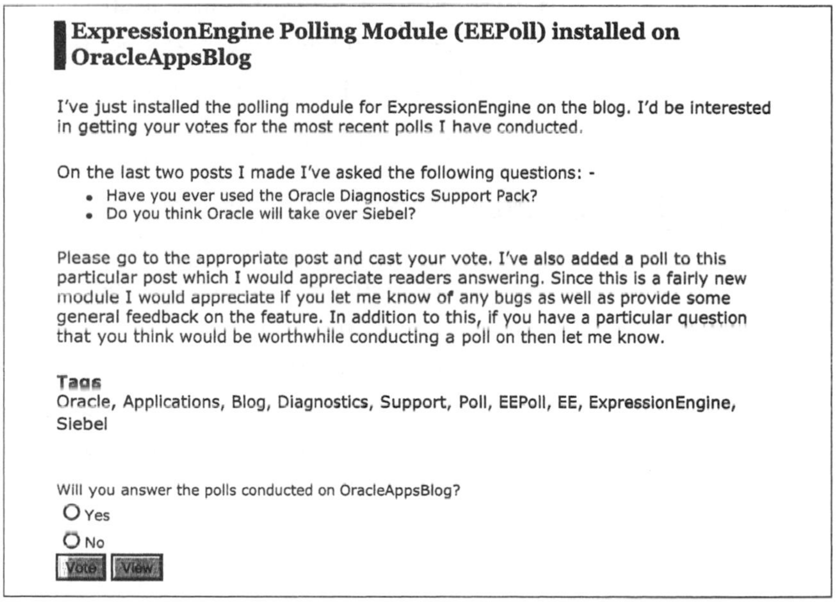

> **ExpressionEngine Polling Module (EEPoll) installed on OracleAppsBlog**
>
> I've just installed the polling module for ExpressionEngine on the blog. I'd be interested in getting your votes for the most recent polls I have conducted.
>
> On the last two posts I made I've asked the following questions: -
> - Have you ever used the Oracle Diagnostics Support Pack?
> - Do you think Oracle will take over Siebel?
>
> Please go to the appropriate post and cast your vote. I've also added a poll to this particular post which I would appreciate readers answering. Since this is a fairly new module I would appreciate if you let me know of any bugs as well as provide some general feedback on the feature. In addition to this, if you have a particular question that you think would be worthwhile conducting a poll on then let me know.
>
> **Tags**
> Oracle, Applications, Blog, Diagnostics, Support, Poll, EEPoll, EE, ExpressionEngine, Siebel
>
> Will you answer the polls conducted on OracleAppsBlog?
> ○ Yes
> ○ No
> [Vote] [View]

In this example, Richard Byrom has implemented a poll on his OracleAppsBlog.

FOLLOW THE BUZZ

Sometimes measurement can generate more than actionable data. It can be downright fun. No measurement activity is more fun that measuring the buzz around an issue—unless, of course, the buzz is negative and aimed at you! Either way, there are enough tools available to make it easy to find out the degree to which people are talking about your issues and, by extension, how much influence your efforts are having on the nature of that buzz.

BlogPulse, a free service of Intelliseek, offers an easy-to-use tool to measure the buzz around any given topic. By way of example, let's look at a business topic that was hot at the time this book was being written: Apple Computer's introduction of the iPod Nano. Figure 11.5 shows the results when we enter *iPod Nano* into the BlogPulse Trend Search.

In the graph BlogPulse produces, it's easy to see that the biggest buzz around the Nano occurred on the day Apple made the surprise announcement that it was introducing the tiny digital media player, but buzz dropped off precipitously after that. (See Figure 11.6.)

BlogPulse also lets you compare the buzz between two or more items. If a company wants to assess how well its marketing efforts are working in the blogosphere compared to a competitor's, BlogPulse makes it easy. Several anticipated movies were about to be released as we prepared this book for press. One was *A History of Violence* and another was *Corpse Bride*. Which one was getting the most buzz in the blogosphere? (See Figure 11.7.)

FIGURE 11.5 *BlogPulse Trend Monitoring Begins with Entering the Term Around Which You'd Like to Assess Buzz*

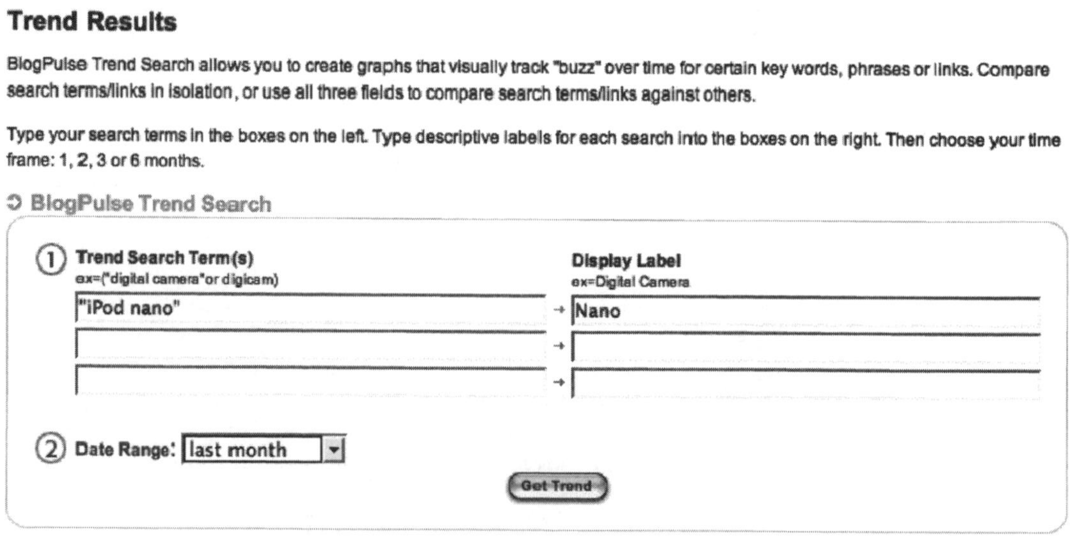

Trend Results

BlogPulse Trend Search allows you to create graphs that visually track "buzz" over time for certain key words, phrases or links. Compare search terms/links in isolation, or use all three fields to compare search terms/links against others.

Type your search terms in the boxes on the left. Type descriptive labels for each search into the boxes on the right. Then choose your time frame: 1, 2, 3 or 6 months.

↻ BlogPulse Trend Search

① **Trend Search Term(s)**
ex=("digital camera" or digicam)

Display Label
ex=Digital Camera

"iPod nano" → Nano

→

→

② **Date Range:** last month ▾

(Get Trend)

Source: © Intelliseek, Inc. All Rights Reserved.

FIGURE 11.6 *BlogPulse Returns a Chart to Show the Ebb and Flow of Buzz around the Topic Requested*

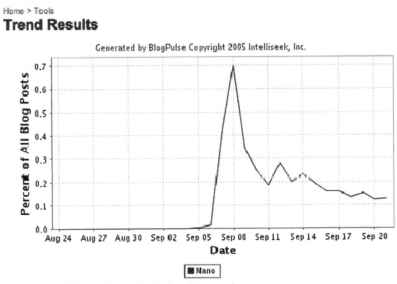

Source: © Intelliseek, Inc. All Rights Reserved.

FIGURE 11.7 *BlogPulse Also Allows You to Compare Buzz between Two or More Items*

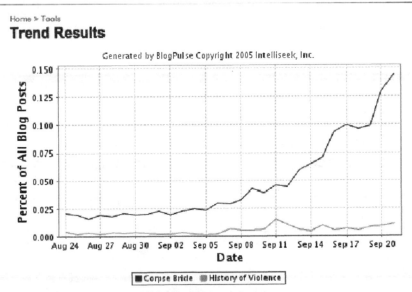

Source: © Intelliseek, Inc. All Rights Reserved.

Tim Burton probably could have felt pretty good about the box office his movie would generate going head-to-head on its opening weekend with a movie that had generated early Oscar talk.

Incidentally, BlogPulse also offers up the topics generating the *most* buzz in a number of categories, including news, politics, sports, entertainment, business, science and technology, and other categories.

Of course, BlogPulse is not the sole free service you can use to monitor buzz. Most of the blog search engines let you set up searches for keywords. You could simply set up a search using any of your company's brands or marks to see what bloggers and others posting comments are saying. Assign a score to each post and comment you find; a score of five indicates a very positive reference while a one represents a very negative reference. Tally the scores at the end of the month to determine the average score. Then, take whatever action you were planning (e.g., a new series of posts on an existing blog or the launch of a new blog), then repeat the exercise to see if you have been able to affect the tone of conversation in the blogosphere. If you can demonstrate that your blogging efforts are influencing perceptions, then you have proven the effectiveness of your blogging efforts.

SURVEYS

Some of the measurement tools that have worked on traditional Web sites work equally well on blogs. There is, for example, no reason you cannot employ a random pop-up (or "roadblock") survey. These surveys can appear on every tenth visit to the blog (or whatever frequency you choose). The survey asks the visitor to take a minute to assess the blog. These requests for input work best when the company offers some kind of incentive. One pharmaceutical company, for instance, offered a free copy of a heart-healthy cookbook in exchange for completing a brief survey about the effectiveness of its site dedicated to a cardiac medicine.

MEDIA PLACEMENT

For better and worse, some of your company's blog posts will find their way into the mainstream media. Because somebody in your organization probably is already monitoring media coverage, it should be no problem to add this new dimension to the monitoring effort. Every reference that was derived from a blog post should be identified and then assessed for its tone (positive, neutral, or negative), the aspect of the company addressed (brand or mark, corporate, customer service, etc.), format (newspaper, TV, magazine, etc.), and reach. You could conceivably assign a dollar equivalent for each placement based on what the publication or TV station would charge for an ad of the same size. We don't recommend this approach, because it presumes that the values of advertising and editorial placement are equal—and they are not. Still, if management is breathing down your neck for some quantifiable measures, ad equivalents can provide you with some ammunition.

THE SHERLOCK HOLMES EFFECT

The great detective of 210 Baker Street posited that once you eliminate the impossible, whatever remains, no matter how improbable, must be the answer. This deductive theorem applies to blogs as well as anything else. Just ask Paul Woodhouse, author of The Tinbasher Blog and the leader of Tinpot Alley, a U.K. metalworking shop that produces stainless steel planters and other items. Woodhouse was one of the first business leaders to blog, and he credits the blog with an increase in visibility and business.

There is no measurement that can prove that Tinbasher caused the boost to the company's reputation and bottom line but, as Holmes said, if nothing else could account for it—no new advertising, no sudden insatiable demand for stainless steel planters sweeping the British Isles—then the blog *had* to have something to do with it.

"Since revamping my little blog in October, I've been truly astonished by its impact on a myriad of levels," Woodhouse wrote in a comment posted to another blog. "In fact, if I'm being honest, everything the 'theoretical' business bloggers ram down everybody's throat is perfectly true—and then some.

"It's no longer a case of 'can it work,' but of learning how it works and getting on board. And I, for one, am happy to do my tiny little bit in that respect. I'll happily talk to anyone, anywhere about it purely because I enjoy it and believe in it so fundamentally.

"And believe me, it's possibly one of the simplest things I've managed to set up with regards to our company's Web presence."

Woodhouse obviously enjoys blogging and, to be sure, he's very good at it. But the man *is* responsible for his company's performance. Surely he has more to go on than his passion for blogging in deciding to invest the amount of time he does in the effort. Again, Woodhouse's own words provide the answer.

"It didn't cost a single penny to set up our company blog, but the direct and indirect effects of it have been amazing," he explains. "By indirect effect I'm referring to the boost in search engine placement the main company site has received and therefore people finding us more easily. In turn we're also seeing an increase in enquiries which are also more targeted in terms of what we actually do as a business. The direct effect is people coming through the blog. However you want to look at it, it's all about the blog.

"And how do I know this? Either our customers tell us, or we ask them. I can also look at our stats—the first month of the blog saw double the amount of traffic of the previous two combined. It isn't tricky.

"Before we incorporated a company blog we maybe received three or four enquiries a month. Now we receive at least that a week. They're also better, more focused enquiries that are turning into nice little earners.

"I can only speak from a small business perspective which is operating on an extremely small/non-existent budget. We don't advertise and everything has been done in-house, so to speak. But for our company, it's proven to be better than sliced bread. It's sliced bread and jam."

So Woodhouse's company doesn't advertise, but his inquiries and sales have increased appreciably. Customers tell him the blog influenced their decision and, in the absence of any other reason for the increase in business, Woodhouse (in the best British tradition) surmises that the blog must be responsible.

MEASURING STRATEGICALLY

While you should most definitely measure your blogging efforts, doing so shouldn't be a matter of simply cherry-picking from the methods listed in this chapter. What you measure should depend primarily on what you're trying to accomplish with your blog and secondarily on measures that will mean something to your organization's leaders. For example, if your goal is to generate buzz around a product launch, measuring search engine placement won't impress anybody. On the other hand, if search engine rankings are important to your boss, you can supplement your measurement of the buzz with the value of the search engine placements you have achieved.

SUMMARY

Having a blog is great, but unless you can measure its effectiveness, you may not be reaping its full benefits. By tapping into the wealth of services available on the World Wide Web—many of them free and easy to use—you can ensure your efforts are reaching your intended audience.

Once your audiences are reading your blog, your messages are reaching them in a manner more likely to produce the desired results than traditional corporate communications ever could.

12

LEGAL CONSIDERATIONS

As with any corporate or business communications, you can expect that your organization's lawyers will want to get involved. Ensuring that your blogs don't cause legal problems is a good idea. Of course, there is risk in *any* communication, and the degree to which you implement legal safeguards should be tempered by weighing the benefits against the risks.

There is, for example, a chance that something posted to a blog could lead an individual to feel they were libeled. In the United States, that individual is free to bring a lawsuit whether or not it is justified. That possibility is no reason not to blog if you have determined that the blog can produce significant value for the organization. A lawyer's job is to point out the exposures to which a blog could open you. Your responsibility, as a business leader, is to assess those exposures and make an informed decision about whether and how to proceed.

In this chapter, we'll cover the primary legal issues you could face and the means by which to reduce or minimize your risk. The

key to avoiding legal problems, though, has nothing at all to do with the technology or format of blogging. It has *everything* to do with *content.* Fundamentally, if every one of your company bloggers simply plays by the rules, you will be exposed to no risk at all. It is the lack of confidence that employees won't make any mistakes or say things they shouldn't that drives most of the legal staff's concerns. Consequently, we'll also offer some proposed policies your organization should implement and communicate to all employees.

Accustomed to reviewing much information the company publishes to the public, your legal staff may insist on reviewing all blog content before it is published. This is a bad idea for a number of reasons. First, it delays the publication of information readers may be awaiting (particularly if it's something like an update on a fast-moving issue). More significant, though, is the language attorneys are likely to want to substitute in any blog post, "legalizing" the tone of the writing. As we've discussed repeatedly, blogs must be written in the genuine, authentic voice of the author, a style easily subverted by legalese. It is better that your bloggers have a thorough understanding of what they can and cannot say and to trust them to abide by the rules.

The higher your blogger ranks in the organization, the less worried your legal team should be. When Bob Lutz, vice chairman of General Motors, announced he would start a blog, GM attorneys initially insisted on reviewing his copy. Lutz stood firm, though, noting that by the time someone achieves the level of vice chairman, they should know what can and cannot be said. The attorneys reluctantly agreed.

The sections of this chapter that follow address the primary kinds of legal issues that could arise from imprudent blog posts. There is far more information available on each of these issues; our intent here is simply to introduce the areas of risk, not to offer a full legal course. Of course, the law and the requirements for ensuring compliance are whatever your organization's general

counsel *says* they are. Be sure to consult with your legal team before undertaking a blogging program.

DISCLOSURE

The concept of disclosure covers a lot of ground but comes down to one basic concept: No representative of your organization can reveal material information to a select audience in violation of regulatory rules.

In the United States, these rules fall under the jurisdiction of the Securities and Exchange Commission (SEC) and what is known as Reg FD, shorthand for a full-disclosure regulation. Fairness is at the heart of Reg FD, which decrees that material information be disclosed concurrently to all interested audiences so that no one group has an unfair investment advantage.

Reg FD reads: "Whenever an issuer, or any person acting on its behalf, discloses any material nonpublic information regarding that issuer or its securities to [certain enumerated persons], the issuer shall make public disclosure of that information . . . simultaneously, in the case of an intentional disclosure; and . . . promptly, in the case of a non-intentional disclosure."

"Material" information is anything that could affect the organization's financial condition, ranging from quarterly earnings results to a new product introduction. When a couple of blogs reported on Apple Computers' new product plans, the computer maker took the extraordinary step of legal action against the bloggers to identify the sources of their information, presumably Apple employees. By leaking the information, those employees violated Reg FD and put Apple at risk. Similar leaks by Sun Microsystems employees led chief technology officer Jonathan Scwhartz to reiterate the importance of following disclosure rules, using his public blog—widely read by employees—to make his appeal.

The policies by which your employees are expected to abide undoubtedly already address disclosure, but the rule should be reiterated in a blog-specific policy.

INTELLECTUAL PROPERTY

Trademark and copyright are the issues in play when we talk about intellectual property—both yours and anybody else's.

While your organization isn't likely to sue itself over trademark or copyright violations, its efforts to protect those intellectual property rights could be undermined if your own employees misuse the marks. Recently, for example, Lego Group—the company that makes those interconnecting plastic brick toys—has made a big deal out of protecting its mark by calling the product Lego toys or Lego bricks rather than pluralizing the word (e.g., Legos). But if an employee or executive blogger began calling them Legos in a blog, a defendant in a trademark action could make the case that he read the plural use of the mark on an official Lego blog. After all, if the company's employees and executives don't make any effort to protect their trademark, why would the general public be held to a higher standard? (Most internal company publications and documents are very careful to adhere to trademarks. At Mattel, no employee would refer to "Barbies," a trademark violation. The trademark is Barbie (singular), so references would be to Barbie dolls. You want to make sure your own employee bloggers respect the company's various brand trademarks and copyrights in order to keep the misuse from spreading.

Of more immediate concern is the violation of someone else's intellectual property. Trademark and copyright laws that govern use of somebody else's intellectual property are exactly the same online as they are in the "real world;" outside of fair use, you must obtain permission in order to use somebody else's work, whether it's text, an image, music, video, or any other content.

Fair use, however, covers a lot of ground. If, for example, you are writing about what somebody else posted on her own blog, you can quote the part of that post you want to talk about without fear of infringing on that blogger's copyright. According to the United States Copyright Act, "fair use . . . for purposes such as criticism, comment, news reporting, teaching (including multiple copies for classroom use), scholarship, or research, is not an infringement of copyright."

There is plenty of material available online that goes into detail on what constitutes fair use. In addition, here are some of the things you *can* do without violating anybody's intellectual property rights:

- Quote government documents
- Report facts and ideas that somebody else wrote about; copyright does not protect facts, only the way they were expressed in a document
- Link to any blog, blog post, site, or page on the World Wide Web

One question that has not been addressed yet by the courts is whether you can be held liable for copyright or trademark violations committed by somebody writing a comment that they leave on your blog. You'll probably have a harder time avoiding this charge in court if you monitor your comments—that is, if you read and approve them before allowing them to appear on your blog—than if anybody can just post a comment without you reading it first.

Creative Commons

There is one additional issue to address when it comes to intellectual property: How much latitude will you allow others should they want to copy something that appeared in *your* blog? Fortunately, there's an easy answer to this one. It's called Creative Commons.

The Creative Commons license is based on a concept introduced by constitutional lawyer and professor Lawrence Lessig. The site offers a simple wizard that lets you establish a license that grants certain permissions for use of your content. By applying the license logo to your blog, anybody can see what they are or are not allowed to do. The licenses are available for 20 different jurisdictions, each one designed to hold up in a court in that country. (Of course, you'll still have to use your own attorneys!) You simply specify whether you'll allow commercial use and whether they may modify your content; you can also require anybody who modifies your content to allow others to do the same with *their* material. You can also indicate whether anybody copying your work must give you credit for the material they're copying. Figure 12.1 shows what the Creative Commons license looks like for Shel's blog. Creative Commons licenses are becoming commonplace on many blogs as a means of articulating the rights you want to grant.

DEFAMATION

Libel and slander are both covered under the idea of defamation. Libel refers to the written word while slander accounts for what is spoken. In both cases, you defame somebody when you make a false and unprivileged statement that can harm the reputation of the person about whom you're talking. It's defamation whether you made the statement with malice or out of negligence.

In the United States, a statement has to pass three tests to be considered defamation:

1. The statement was published to somebody other than the individual who was the subject of the statement. If you send a letter or e-mail just to the individual you're talking

FIGURE 12.1 *A Typical Creative Commons License*

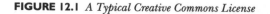

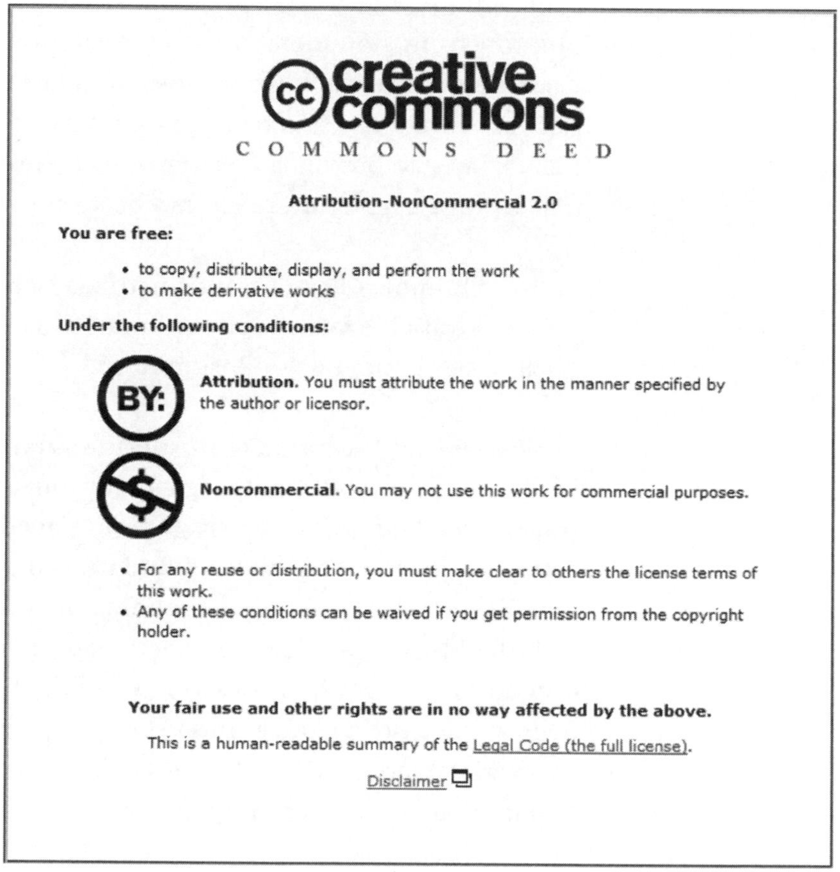

COMMONS DEED

Attribution-NonCommercial 2.0

You are free:

- to copy, distribute, display, and perform the work
- to make derivative works

Under the following conditions:

Attribution. You must attribute the work in the manner specified by the author or licensor.

Noncommercial. You may not use this work for commercial purposes.

- For any reuse or distribution, you must make clear to others the license terms of this work.
- Any of these conditions can be waived if you get permission from the copyright holder.

Your fair use and other rights are in no way affected by the above.

This is a human-readable summary of the Legal Code (the full license).

Disclaimer

about, it's not defamation. Publishing the same statement in a blog, though, clearly satisfies this requirement.

2. The statement is false.
3. It's clear that the statement was about the individual claiming to have been defamed and tends to be harmful to that individual.

If a statement must be false in order to be defamatory, then truth is an absolute defense against a defamation claim. Even then, however, you could be in for some trouble because proving what is true could be a challenge. Also, you're entitled to state your opinion, but it takes a lawyer to separate what is a genuine opinion from statements that were simply labeled as opinion. Courts tend to use the "reasonable" standard: Would a reasonable person hearing the statement think it was opinion or a statement that claimed to present a "verifiable fact" (one that can be proved true or false)? The difference can be seen in these examples:

> Opinion: "I can't stand anything Jackie Collins writes."
> Verifiable fact: "In my opinion, CEO John Smith has been looting Acme, Inc.'s pension fund."

There is an exception to the definition of defamation. A public figure has to prove that you actually *wanted* to harm him when you defamed him, while a private figure need only prove that you acted negligently. This higher standard is harder to prove.

One issue that is still in limbo as of this writing is whether you, the blogger, are liable for defamatory comments somebody else posts to your blog. A case was in litigation as this book was being written over precisely this issue. It is generally agreed, though, that you are more likely to be held liable if you monitor your comments—that is, you read them before authorizing them to appear on your blog.

RIGHT TO PRIVACY

In the United States, the right to privacy is held very dear. As far as the law is concerned, a private fact is simply one that an individual hasn't made public. If you "out" somebody on a blog post, disclosing that he or she is gay, that qualifies as an intrusion into seclusion; you have violated that individual's privacy. As soon as the individual discloses that fact, though, it moves into the pub lic domain and you won't get into any trouble for writing about it—at least, not from the law!

Not all states allow someone to sue for publication of a private fact, and those that do are not consistent in how the law is addressed. California, for example, requires that four facts be shown before a lawsuit is merited: *public disclosure* of a *private fact* that is *offensive to a reasonable person* and which is *not a legitimate matter of public concern.* That last criterion is important, because if a private fact is newsworthy, then California allows it.

The question, then, becomes: What is newsworthy? As you might expect by now, the courts leave this to the "reasonable person" standard. It's newsworthy, therefore, if some reasonable members of the community could find a legitimate interest in the information.

There is one additional dimension of privacy to cover: intrusion into seclusion. This occurs when you intrude into the privacy or seclusion of one's private affairs or concerns (again, assuming a reasonable person would find the intrusion offensive).

FIRED FOR BLOGGING

The news has been filled in recent years with accounts of companies firing employees for what they have published in their private, personal blogs. Perhaps the best known case is that of Ellen Simonetti, a former Delta Air Lines flight attendant. She included some photos of herself in her blog, Queen of the Skies. In these photos Simonetti wore her flight attendant's uniform while striking some mildly suggestive poses. Delta fired her, an action she has been fighting ever since. But Simonetti is not alone. Google fired newly hired Mark Jen for an innocuous post to his blog; he was later hired by another company based in large part on his blogging abilities. Web developer Joyce Park was fired from Friendster for blogging. In the United Kingdom, a bookstore employee of

Waterstone's was fired for making disparaging remarks about his boss; a competing bookseller later hired him for a better position—again, in part because he understood the world of blogs.

These are just some of the high-profile cases in which companies have terminated employees for what they have written in their personal blogs. (Getting fired for blogging is often referred to as being "Dooced," a reference to a blog called Dooce.com, owned by Heather Armstrong, who was fired for blogging in 2002.) None of these cases needed to happen. It is, in fact, in a company's best interest to avoid firing anybody for blogging. Generally, anybody terminated for writing a blog is viewed by the public as something of a rock star, a hero of the masses. Meanwhile, the company that fired the individual is viewed as a villain, a cold, heartless, and clueless organization that just does not "get it."

SUMMARY

Blogs can cause your organization legal trouble in a number of ways, ranging from libel to trademark violation, from leaks to regulatory violations. Of course, the same legal woes exist in a number of other communication channels, including e-mail, Web sites, and even faxes and photocopies. Most legal issues can be addressed by establishing and communicating policies, and explaining why these policies have been implemented. There is no reason to forgo the benefits your organization can realize from a blog just because of an unreasonable fear of legal issues. Plenty of organizations with tenacious legal departments have still been able to take advantage of the benefits the blogosphere has to offer.

Chapter

13

THE FUTURE
OF BLOGGING

Blogs are a communication channel. They
are one of many communication channels available, all of which
have their uses. Many pundits have decried that blogs signal the
end of the mainstream media, press releases, or any number of established communications. Quite simply, they are wrong! Blogs
are complementary to the pre-existing communications channels
available. In fact, if this is indeed the Information Age as often
claimed, it will be marked by an increasing array of complementary communications channels and choices. In this chapter we
will look at the future of blogging, including podcasting and
video blogging.

New media do not, with rare exceptions, utterly replace old
media. However, old media learn to adapt, and sometimes shrink
as a result of the competition. Many people expected television to
replace radio, for example. Instead, content best suited for the
visual medium migrated to television and content best *heard*
filled radio's available bandwidth and radio continued to thrive.

Similarly, today traditional media will survive but adapt in the face of consumer-generated content like blogs. The arguments against the press release are valid to a degree, and blogs may be used to accomplish many of the tasks that would have been applied to a press release in the past. However, a press release remains the ultimate, official statement of record by an organization, and is recognized as such by institutions including the press and the courts. So, while there may be less use of press releases, they won't vanish altogether.

"The future is now" is not exactly correct. "The future starts now" is more in the right direction. Forecasting the future is quite simply impossible. Although we can look with fair certainty at what is likely to occur in the short term, which might be defined as up to a few months or very few years, the long term, say two years and further out, is anyone's guess. Who would have guessed the Internet would change shopping forever? Certainly not Ted, despite having been on the Internet for over 25 years. Who can predict where podcasting is going and what, if anything, it might revolutionize? Certainly not Shel, despite being a pioneering podcaster. That said, some fairly intelligent guesses, or estimates if you prefer, can be made.

Most blogs look quite similar to each other. Surveys have shown that a typical blog is not very user friendly. Users not familiar with blogs are often confused by the various components, especially trackbacks. One study, from Catalyst Design Group, introduced a blog to regular Web users who didn't already read blogs. The study concluded:

- Most participants couldn't figure out how to navigate around the blog and were confused by the different sections (categories, trackbacks, etc.)
- There was no clear understanding about how commenting worked. Would comments appear immediately? Require approval? Result in an answer?

- Every single participant agreed that RSS was confusing, and that blogs don't help aid in the understanding of what RSS is, how it works, or why they should use it.
- When starting on a lower-level page, participants were unclear about what the purpose of a home page might be or what they would find there.

At the end of the session, participants said they liked the blog and would be inclined to read more, but complained that blogs don't offer enough assistance to newcomers to help them figure out the various elements and how to use them.

Understanding comments, where they come from, and how to leave them can cause significant confusion. Ted recently experienced extreme frustration at trying to leave a comment on a well-known blog; to say it was user-unfriendly would be an understatement! The overall design of blogs can use a radical change to something more intuitive and user friendly. More familiarity with blogs is not the answer; we need to change the look and feel of blogs, not potential blog readers! In time, blogs will become easier for the layperson, just as, hopefully, all technology, including computers and related software, will become easier to use.

Most business do not blog today. Most businesses do not monitor the blogosphere today. The number of businesses that do, and gain benefits, is growing steadily. Businesses do not need a blog department, chief blogging officer, or some similar title. Businesses *do* need to integrate blogging into their already existing communications infrastructure. Many of those that have are already reaping significant benefits. As the importance and influence of blogging grows, those that do not will be at a disadvantage. Just as an organization that chooses to ignore an important communication channel such as print newspapers is to some extent impaired, organizations that ignore the blogosphere will be missing an important source of information and feedback about the organization, its industry, its people, and more. All organizations of any significant size can and will benefit. The corner gas station may choose not to, but your child's lemonade stand may: imagine the business a post in a community blog might generate.

Web sites are starting to take on the charactcristics of blogs. Some are allowing users to leave comments. Some Web sites have implemented a reverse-chronological-ordered list of "what's new" or something similar on their home pages. Blogs are also becoming more complex. Some blogging software, for example Radio UserLand, allows bloggers to create arbitrary Web pages that can be used for anything, just as Web authoring software does. Although Web authoring software and blogging software are distinct today, there will be software available in the future that can do both well.

PODCASTS

Podcasts are more than just audio blogs as wc've mentioned. A podcast is an audio blog where the audio posts have a show-like structure that can be subscribed to and automatically downloaded. Podcasts occupy a special niche compared to ordinary blogs and vlogs (video blogs), which are discussed below. Podcasts can be consumed at times that reading or watching video would be impossible or inadvisable, for example while driving, exercising, or cooking. Podcasts are not tied to a computer; they are commonly downloaded to iPods and other digital music devices as well as burned onto CDs, making podcasts convenient for listening to anywhere.

Podcasting and podcasts are often compared to radio and radio shows; however, this is a limiting description. Podcasts will eventually occupy most or all of the niches that radio does, but they have more potential. Radio is expensive; it needs a certain number of listeners to make it financially viable, and there is a limited range of radio spectrum available. This limits the range of topics radio can cover. Podcasts in contrast are stunningly cheap to produce, use no limited resources such as radio spectrum, and can therefore cover niche areas that would not be viable for radio shows. Anyone with a PC, a $10 microphone, and a place to host audio files can start podcasting almost immediately.

Adam Curry is widely credited as creating the first podcast in August 2004. Curry also developed the first "podcatcher," software that did for podcasts what feedreaders did for text. That software, iPodder, was enabled by a concurrent development, the release of RSS 2.0, developed by coder Dave Winer, who added the ability to distribute media files (like MP3 audio files) in an RSS feed.

Now there are over 15,000 podcasts, a number that will be woefully out of date by the time that you read this because over 500 new podcasts are started every week! Most podcasts seem to be in the entertainment category, and entertainment can be big business, of course. There are also several podcasts being produced by businesses, and their numbers are also increasing rapidly. For example, Reuters, *Business Week,* Disney, General Motors, Purina, IBM, Virgin Atlantic, NASA, and Cisco Systems, to name but a few, are producing podcasts. Quite simply, podcasts are exploding in terms of number and listenership. The term sometimes used by podcasters is "drinking the podcasting Kool-Aid®," to refer to podcasting converts. Podcasting is an addictive medium.

However, podcasting is simply another medium, another channel to communicate with customers, potential customers, investors, employees, and others. It has strengths and weaknesses when compared to traditional blogs, and these will become more obvious as time progresses. For example, podcasts are hard to browse, although show notes—text descriptions that accompany the audio files—help in this regard. And software under development, such as Podscope, *will* be able to search the content of audio.

Podcasts, as we've mentioned before, can be listened to at times when reading a blog is inadvisable, such as while driving. One of the strengths of blogs—their personal and conversational nature—is even stronger with podcasts, as the following e-mail from Ted to Shel illustrates (posted to Ted's blog with Shel's permission):

To: Shel Holtz
From: Ted Demopoulos
Subject: your podcast—I now know you 182% better

Just listened to your latest podcast at <u>forimmediaterelease.biz</u>—great job!

What impressed me the most, is not how interesting and professional it is, but how personal it is. We've communicated a bit through blogs and email, but hearing you directly with my ears bumped up the "I know Shel" feeling several notches. Some of this is probably because you are conversing with Neville in your podcast, but much of it is from simply hearing your voice.

Occasionally people tell me they feel they know me through my blog.
Podcasting clearly has the ability to bring that to another level.

Podcasting and blogging do not have to be mutually exclusive. They are different communications channels, and either, both, or sometimes neither may be appropriate for specific applications and uses.

VLOGS

The term *vlog* is short for video blog, a blog in which the primary content is video. A vlog—also sometimes called a *vidcast*—usually includes supporting text, and a screen shot to represent each video. Most vlogs use RSS to allow users to subscribe (taking advantage of freeware software like Fireant), and the video content is represented similarly to audio in podcasts—as the same RSS "enclosures" that enable podcasts. The videos tend to be short clips, and the quality can range from extremely amateurish to professional. We will restrain ourselves from strictly defining vlogging, as even dedicated vloggers strenuously debate the actual definition or whether there even should be a definition for a medium that is so new and evolving.

Recording video, and producing vlogs, is within reach of anyone today—an inexpensive camera can be added to a Windows or Macintosh computer, many digital cameras can take video, some cell phones can take video, or a full professional video team with multiple cameras and professional editing equipment can used.

Video always had a high barrier to entry. Producing remotely professional video was always extremely expensive; the professional quality equipment used to film and then edit the video was out of range for most people. Once a video was produced, distribution was a significant barrier. Although high-end professional equipment is still expensive, in general these barriers no longer exist.

Just as iPods and other digital music players make consuming podcasts anywhere possible, portable "video players" will do the same for vlogs. The obvious choice today is a cell phone, many of which have integrated video screens and storage, and whose video capabilities are evolving and improving rapidly.

We haven't seen any business vlogs yet, although just as political blogs are quite common and extremely popular, political vlogs are sprouting. North Carolina Senator John Edwards receives and responds to questions using video on his vlog. Boston, Massachusetts, city council member John Tobin also has a vlog. Entertainment companies are also tapping into the idea; director Peter Jackson produced a vlog during the production of his motion picture remake of *King Kong*. Certainly, business vlogs can't be far behind, and it doesn't require much imagination to see potential uses. Speeches to investors in a company, how-to videos focusing on a company's products, CEO updates, and others are some potential uses.

Rocketboom represents another use of vidcasts. A daily three-minute entertainment-focused newscast, Rocketboom features an anchorwoman in a newsroom set. The same approach (without the sarcasm and political point of view) could be embraced as a means of communicating news about an organization, an issue, a product, and a host of other topics. Internally, employees would be far more inclined to watch a daily (or even weekly) vidcast that summarizes company news than to sit at their desks (with their copious free time) and read the text news stories on the intranet.

WHERE ARE THESE ALL HEADING?

So where are these new media—blogs, podcasts, vlogs—heading? As we've mentioned, it is impossible to predict the future, but some things are evident.

Blogs have exploded in popularity and podcasts are now exploding. Both are making significant inroads into business, and blogs are already at the point that businesses can no longer ignore them. Podcasts appear not to be far behind. Vlogs, a much newer medium now populated to some extent by talented eccentrics, will also follow.

These new media are integrating into culture and business. The term *blog* will probably disappear in the future, along with *podcast* and *vlog*. They will be considered amusing anachronistic terms, like *zoot suit, power tie,* and *new economy.* Their usage in business will be a given, just as essentially all businesses use computers and telephones today.

The "business" of blogging, podcasting, and vlogging, which we define loosely as their use for profit, where there is no underlying business being supported or promoted, will continue to grow. Profit models will undoubtedly emerge. The Internet began as 100 percent free and noncommercial. Most information on the Internet is still free, although there is certainly content today supported by advertising or only available by purchase. Most blogs, podcasts, and vlogs, or whatever terms we may be using in a few years, will still be free, although some content will be available by subscription or other payment mode. They will not "kill" print media, radio, or television, although these will change significantly in the next few years, just as they have in the past few years.

We are looking forward to going along for the ride! We hope you are too. One thing is certain: businesses can gain a competitive advantage by being early adopters of these new media; if you wait until everyone else does it, you will be at a competitive disadvantage. Our recommendations are clear: businesses need to be involved in the blogosphere today, and that includes, at an absolute minimum, monitoring blogs and keeping an eye on podcasts and vlogs.

Share the message!

Bulk discounts
Discounts start at only 10 copies and range from 30% to 55% off retail price based on quantity.

Custom publishing
Private label a cover with your organization's name and logo. Or, tailor information to your needs with a custom pamphlet that highlights specific chapters.

Ancillaries
Workshop outlines, videos, and other products are available on select titles.

Dynamic speakers
Engaging authors are available to share their expertise and insight at your event.

Call Kaplan Publishing Corporate Sales at
1-800-621-9621, ext. 4511,
or e-mail nakia_hinkle@kaplan.com

KAPLAN) PUBLISHING